MEDIA ENGAGEMENT

Written with media students in mind, this accessible book provides both students and researchers with a new perspective on how to research engagement, not as a metric but as a marker of power relations.

This book navigates the reader through a tighter analytical notion of engagement within an understanding of media, culture and democracy. Dahlgren and Hill offer a new definition of engagement as an energising internal force, and as such a powerful means to further human agency. From this definition, the book builds a generative theory of engagement as a nexus of relations we make and break with media on a daily basis, with examples from political activism, news and disinformation, and the global pandemic. Dahlgren and Hill identify five parameters of engagement in order to understand the relations we have with media across changing public and mediated spheres. This new perspective offers students and researchers pathways for investigating the meaning of media engagement as a resource for living.

It will be particularly useful for undergraduate courses on media audiences and publics, political communication and democracy, media and cultural theory, journalism, and for media, communication and sociology studies more broadly.

Peter Dahlgren is Professor Emeritus of Media and Communication at Lund University, Sweden. Along with many works on public spheres, civic cultures and media theory, his publications include *Media and Political Engagement* (2009) and *The Political Web* (2013).

Annette Hill is Professor of Media and Communication at Lund University, Sweden, and Visiting Professor at King's College London. Her latest book is *The Handbook of Mobile Socialities* (with M. Hartmann and M. Andersson) and her next book is *Roaming Audiences* (2023).

KEY IDEAS IN MEDIA AND CULTURAL STUDIES

The *Key Ideas in Media and Cultural Studies* series covers the main concepts, issues, debates and controversies in contemporary media and cultural studies. Titles in the series constitute authoritative, original essays rather than literary surveys, but are also written explicitly to support undergraduate teaching. The series provides students and teachers with lively and original treatments of key topics in the field.

Cultural Policy
David Bell and Kate Oakley

Reality TV
Annette Hill

Culture
Ben Highmore

Representation
Jenny Kidd

Celebrity
Sean Redmond

Global Cultural Economy
Christiaan De Beukelaer and Kim-Marie Spence

Marxism
Karl Marx's Fifteen Key Concepts for Cultural and Communication Studies
Christian Fuchs

Deep Mediatization
Andreas Hepp

Information
Micky Lee

Media Engagement
Peter Dahlgren and Annette Hill

For more information about this series, please visit: www.routledge.com/Key-Ideas-in-Media–Cultural-Studies/book-series/KEYIDEA

MEDIA ENGAGEMENT

Peter Dahlgren and Annette Hill

Routledge
Taylor & Francis Group

LONDON AND NEW YORK

Cover image: J.C. Lee

First published 2023
by Routledge
4 Park Square, Milton Park, Abingdon, Oxon OX14 4RN

and by Routledge
605 Third Avenue, New York, NY 10158

Routledge is an imprint of the Taylor & Francis Group, an informa business

© 2023 Peter Dahlgren and Annette Hill

British Library Cataloguing-in-Publication Data
A catalogue record for this book is available from the British Library

Library of Congress Cataloging-in-Publication Data
Names: Dahlgren, Peter, 1946- author. | Hill, Annette, author.
Title: Media engagement / Peter Dahlgren and Annette Hill.
Description: Abingdon, Oxon ; New York, NY : Routledge, 2023. |
Series: Key ideas in media and cultural studies |
Includes bibliographical references and index.
Identifiers: LCCN 2022016794 (print) | LCCN 2022016795 (ebook) |
ISBN 9781032016603 (hardback) | ISBN 9781032016610 (paperback) |
ISBN 9781003179481 (ebook)
Subjects: LCSH: Mass media–Social aspects. | Mass media–Political aspects. |
Mass media and culture. | Social action. | Political participation.
Classification: LCC HM1206 .D344 2023 (print) |
LCC HM1206 (ebook) | DDC 302.23–dc23/eng/20220502
LC record available at https://lccn.loc.gov/2022016794
LC ebook record available at https://lccn.loc.gov/2022016795

ISBN: 978-1-032-01660-3 (hbk)
ISBN: 978-1-032-01661-0 (pbk)
ISBN: 978-1-003-17948-1 (ebk)

DOI: 10.4324/9781003179481

Typeset in Times New Roman
by Newgen Publishing UK

Contents

ILLUSTRATIONS

FOREWORD

I am very pleased to write a Foreword for this book, not only because of the importance of its theme but also because I have followed the widely cited writings of its two authors for many years and very much welcome the way that their distinctive perspectives and analytic skills are productively brought together here.

It is widely noted that the term 'engagement' can cover a range of circumstances both in relation to social action and individual subjectivity. Ideas of orientation, involvement, attachment and participation are variously activated in what is sometimes a vocabulary of overlapping terms. As far as matters of communication are concerned, questions of perception, recognition, interpretation and evaluation become pertinent within what are often complex linkages. In both cases, the diversity and overlaps are part of what this book explores.

The terms, extent and nature of *political engagement* have posed key questions for political structures and civic society over centuries, inscribed within very different national histories. However, the multiple forms of what we now call 'the media' have clearly introduced radically new conditions for almost all lines of social and political engagement. They have done this through the way that their flows of information and entertainment have themselves become a key focus of regular engagement by audiences and users. This kind of engagement is active on 'both sides', as it were, because media have increasingly employed diverse strategic approaches to 'target' and to 'win' users against increased competition within the modern attention economy. Once 'won', the subsequent alignments often work to position people's perceptions in relation to the broad varieties of social and political engagement currently active in their societies. They offer evaluations of relative worth and benefit, including by appeal to the imagination.

What to pay attention to and what not? What to think and what to feel? What to be for and what against? And in relation to decisions here – what information to trust and what models of citizen behaviour to use as a guide in situations increasingly heavy with both crude and sophisticated forms of disinformation?

Essentially, these are all issues about that most basic and general of terms, sharing some of the same space as 'engagement', *connection*. Here, the connection between individuals and publics, as brokered by the use of different media flows, is a core relationship, one that both impacts upon the patterns and strengths of other connections and is itself strongly shaped by them.

Levels of optionality, flexibility and trust are essential to the development of forms of productive public-individual connections, of how people feel themselves *placed* with respect to their broader societies and how they would like to *place themselves* within them, whether by solidarity, dialogue or dissent. However, the opportunity to make use of civic space in this way, to be 'active' within it, is heavily if variously foreclosed in many countries by strongly commercial strategies grounded in corporate interests or by forms of authoritarian direction. Sometimes by a combination of both. Among other things, this book explores varying circumstances of this kind of 'deficit' at the levels of political system, media flow and, most importantly, individual understanding and feeling. In doing so, it also considers what kinds of response might open up, if only marginally, new possibilities, perhaps via an initial disengagement with the existing pattern.

I like the way that Dahlgren and Hill productively push the idea of 'engagement' a good bit further than self-evident usages, alert to the variations and complexities that their analysis brings out and keen to examine the significance of the dynamics of individual subjectivity in everyday life. The historical and theoretical overview of individual-public-political links that they develop is a concise guide to key transitions and related ideas. It is a notable move in a book of this kind for them then to turn to closely worked case studies of engagement and disengagement in very different national settings. There is an internationalism to the whole approach here, which will surely add to the appeal and take-up of this book.

Only one recommendation can be made to the reader at the end of a Foreword to a book with this title – engage!

John Corner

ACKNOWLEDGEMENTS

Along the way, we have to thank various people for their encouragement, exchange of ideas and fulsome support for thinking through, worrying over and figuring out media engagement.

These include Jeanette Steemers, for co-hosting the Media Engagement and Experiences symposium at the University of Westminster 2016, and for co-editing the special issue on *Media Industry Engagement* for the *Media Industries* journal, including the support of the editors we worked with for that issue. That event was co-organised with Tina Askanius and Jose Luis Urueta, and funded by the Marianne and Marcus Wallenberg Foundation in association with Media Experiences project. Speakers at that event included Douglas Wood (then Group Director of Research and Insight, EndemolShineGroup), Professor Jane Roscoe (Head of the London Film School) and Julie Donovan (Formats Consultant), which resulted in an interview published in the *Media Industries* special issue. Other speakers included Professor Göran Bolin (Södertörn University, Sweden), Professor Raymond Boyle (Glasgow University, UK), Professor John Corner (Leeds University, UK), Dr. Paul Torre (University of Northern Iowa, USA) and Professor Anne Marit Waade (Aarhus University, Denmark) who all contributed to early ideas on media engagement. We also thank the co-organisers of the Media Engagement International Symposium in 2015 at Lund University, March 2015 (Tina Askanius, Sanchari De and Michael Rubsamen), an event funded by Marcus Wallenberg International Symposium Fund.

We also thank the MKV collective and the postgraduate students for the MSc International Programme in Media and Communication at Lund University for their willingness to help run events, debate ideas and reflect on research whilst sharing a meal at Govindas. It goes without saying that this vegetarian restaurant has been the space for some wonderful food and good conversations.

We are indebted to Professor John Corner and Professor Joke Hermes for their kind and constructive comments on early ideas for media engagement, and for numerous inspiring public and private talks on what matters. Thank you to Ignas Kalpokas for their constructive comments on Chapter 7. We would like to thank Simon Dawes for their critical input and support in the publication of the journal article 'The Parameters of Media Engagement' in *Media Theory*, autumn 2020. Parts of the original article can be found in the writings for Chapter 1, Chapter 2 and Chapter 4.

A special thank you goes to J.C. Lee and Trang Nguyen Ha Linh for their research work, generosity and good spirit – the chapters on news engagement are enriched by your interviews, reflections and subtle knowledge. A huge thank you to all the people who gave their time and reflected on their news engagement; it is humbling to listen and learn from these interviews. Thanks also goes to the professionals who were interviewed for the wrestling and populism example, and to Jose Luis Urueta for help with some of the interviews conducted at a live event in Stockholm.

To Karin, as ever.

To the Dahlgrens, a family like no other. To Peter Ullgren, a brighter world with you in it.

Part I

MAPPING ENGAGEMENT

1

INTRODUCTION
UNDERSTANDING MEDIA ENGAGEMENT

On engagement: 'my phone is my greatest friend, my most precious friend'.

One story sets the scene for our book. This young Malaysian's lyrical ode to their phone as 'my greatest friend, my most precious friend' characterises their media engagement as relational. Alongside YouTube and social media, this person turns to Netflix whenever they need a companion (see Figure 1.1). For example, they have a nightly media ritual when ordering food at a restaurant; glancing at YouTube videos whilst waiting, they watch one episode of a television series when their meal arrives, eating slowly to ensure their food and drama end together. This smartphone friendship comes at a cost. It may be their personal phone but household subscriptions for their devices, Wi-Fi and various streaming platforms and cable channels are shared across a familial group; a cousin could be watching Netflix from a shared account, a parent could be watching national television news distributed through a shared cable contract. Thus, personal individual engagement with their smartphone is contingent on material conditions, a form of collective social engagement that is attuned to extended family economics, intergenerational households, intragenerational relationships and regional communications infrastructures.

DOI: 10.4324/9781003179481-2

Figure 1.1 'Smartphone friendship' © 2017 Zaki Habibi/Photograph by Zaki Habibi

This young Malaysian is more than aware that Netflix, their nightly dinner companion, is at the top of the digital platform monopoly, usurping the prime position of national cable and public television in Malaysia as the digital subscription of choice for younger generations. For example, when asked to characterise Netflix, this person described it as an arms dealer: 'basically, you're paying the arms dealer, he has everything, all the guns that you want'. Their rhetorical tactic is a meme in the making – guns and rifles overlaid with films and series, signifying 'weapons of mass distraction'. Think of the *John Wick* film franchise (director Chad Stahleski 2014–2022) and scenes showing bespoke armouries in luxury hotels; in this analogy, Netflix arms their subscribers, creating the illusion of a powerful dealer in entertainment content that is uncensored and available outside the bounds of national television. Indeed, their engagement profile on this platform, typically referred to as an audience metric, tracks their content choices, algorithmically predicts their engagement patterns and aggregates this into a data archive within a closed system of subscriber information. Netflix, 'the arms dealer', also signifies how audience engagement has been weaponised by contemporary capitalist media.

This book grows out of an article (Dahlgren and Hill 2020), which was an intervention into the way media industries have captured engagement in commercial logics. Terms such as consumer engagement or social media engagement are strategically designed to drive media markets. From the perspective of media industries, engagement has largely been treated as a behavioural feature that can be measured, with the aim of enhanced success in targeting and reaching consumers. This perspective of media engagement prioritises the here and now; it is the moment of engagement that is given value, whether this is in the form of attention or affective investment. And the most powerful discourses surrounding media engagement emanate from within media industries and commercial sectors: this is a more traditional valuation of audiences and their attention, consumer trends and social media analytics, which places emphasis on engagement as a commodity.

As a counterpoint to this horizon, we define media engagement as an energising internal force that propels citizens to participate in society. We understand media engagement as a dynamic relational process, rooted in affect and identity. With this in mind, engagement analytically becomes inexorably intertwined with affect, and also, it retains a link with rationality. Indeed, to some extent, media engagement can be understood as a playing out of the tension between cognition and affect. Moreover, we distinguish engagement from participation: we see engagement as a subjective prerequisite for participation – which we in turn treat as observable action, the fulfilment of engagement. It is precisely the turn toward subjectivity that makes engagement available for critical analysis of media, in particular, for research interventions that seek to identify injustice, understand resilience, or enhance social and cultural equality. Throughout the chapters of this book, we explore affective connections that generate tonal qualities to media engagement, in particular, in our case studies on public knowledge and social movements during the COVID-19 crisis.

In the last pages of Des Freedman's book on media power, he calls on researchers to 'highlight those dimensions and practices which are crucial in shaping power', in particular, audiences and their 'contradictory consciousness' (Freedman 2014: 146). This book starts with engagement as a place of power relations. Engagement is a site of systemic power within media industries and policies, a site of symbolic power within information and entertainment flows experienced by audiences themselves, and a site of social power where interactions with family and friends, at work or home, in cities and rural areas, are enacted and contested on a daily basis. Engagement involves differential resources. Thus, distinct from the media industry's reductive operationalisation of engagement to capture social media analytics and ratings performance, our approach frames media engagement in democratic and inclusive values by critically considering notions of power and social and digital (in)equalities. It does not require a large analytic leap to grasp that media engagement plays a central role in the dynamics of democracy, public and mediated spheres and citizens' involvement with politics – understood in terms of conflict both in the political formal arena (typified by elections), as well as in the broader societal terrain where all types of contestations of power relations can take place.

MEDIA ENGAGEMENT AS RELATIONAL

We take inspiration from work by Doreen Massey (1994: 149) on place as relational, involving social interactions in, around and beyond a geographical place itself. Her argument regarding power geometry highlights how the relational aspects of place involve differential power, from those who are able to move freely, to those who hold power over others, in some cases effectively imprisoning people, restricting their (im)mobilities. David Morley (2021) also draws on differential relations with media and communications infrastructures and practices; for Morley, it is vital to research both material and virtual dimensions of media in context in order to critically address questions of power.

Our engagement with media is relational; just as mobility and movement is relational, or place and space is relational, so too is engagement made up of differential relations with media and communications systems, sociocultural contexts and everyday practices of audiences. We engage and disengage with media all the time, swiping from one app to another, switching from one television channel to another, tuning into one radio station over another and moving back and forth between entertainment and social media platforms. The spatial terms of 'movement' and 'flow' across platforms and stations alert us to differential power relations, not least those built into the political economy and architecture of the technologies. The communications infrastructures implied in platforms, stations and channels are suggestive of transportation, as Morley points out (2017). Our ability to move across these media places, or to be fixed in one place, positions us as audiences-citizens-users in a power geometry where the owners of regional, national and transnational communication can, and routinely do, hold power over us. But we also have power to engage and disengage with media content on these platforms and channels. Engagement, then, is a nexus of relations we make and break with traditional and alternative media on a daily basis. By analysing engagement as a nexus of relations, we can 'highlight and evaluate the dimensions and practices' of engagement as crucial in shaping the contradictions of media power (Freedman 2014: 146).

Our engagement with media is contingent on material conditions (e.g. money, access and time). These material conditions are in turn contingent on other contextual factors (e.g. digital platforms, mobility and communications infrastructures, crises such as a health pandemic). Thus, media engagement is a lens to think through multiple contingencies, for example, unequal access to economic resources, transportation, or healthcare and education, which are interconnected with dominant discourses concerning gender, race and diversity, or generations. In later chapters focusing on case studies of media engagement in Southeast Asia, we explore how normative ideas of generational relations in the family household can be shaped, and enforced, by the historical contexts of parental roles, postcolonialism and patriarchy in this region; at the same time, the transregional relations for Malaysia and Vietnam indicate how generational relations are shifting in different ways, for example, how female family members drive engagement with mobile social media news during the COVID-19 crisis. In short, the contexts, processes and relationality of media engagement matters, including, in the above example, social relations in local, transregional and international settings.

Take media engagement with local news on movement restriction orders during the COVID-19 crisis: enmeshed in this example we may find that our access to a news app on our smartphone is dependent on a national service provider, overseen by state regulation. Our personal engagement with the news on our phone can be shared with others;

people in the same social media group may engage emotionally with news, and/or engage critically by fact checking news sources. The news can be relevant that day of engagement, but it will be old news by tomorrow; this means we engage, disengage and re-engage with news every hour or every day until we know enough about lockdown measures to take an informed decision on mobility during the pandemic. These contexts and contingencies will form a basis for our argument about the protean nature of media engagement. We present the conceptual building blocks of our understanding of engagement as a spectrum, shifting in intensities, from positive to negative engagement, and from fleeting to embedded engagement with media over time.

Our engagement with media involves various relations, bonds and ties, as well as resources. We form relations with media representations and imaginaries – for example, watching a television crime drama every Sunday, or rewatching *Friends* (NBC, USA 1994–2004) with friends. We create spatial ties to mobile devices and domestic technologies in the home – for example, the placement of the flat screen television, or the mobile charging station. We sign economic contracts with telecommunications companies and subscription services – for example, one contract for all devices, or several contracts for apps, cable services and broadband delivery. We form civic and political allegiances to community action groups – for example, crowdsourcing hyper local news content. The issues and conflicts we find personally relevant and politically compelling are to a great extent a result of the social and cultural resources we have at hand – most of which are media-related in various ways. Our knowledge, information and strategies for obtaining them; our identity as civic and political actors and the networks that sustain these identities; our repertoires of political skills and practices (mostly of a communicative nature) – all impact on our engagement and hence on our participation. These resources are obviously not evenly spread throughout society, but are shaped by relations of power – which, we should keep in mind, are never static and always in tension.

In this short overview, we have already suggested varying relations with media: temporal-spatial, political-economic, local-global, personal-social, and affective-emotional. These differential relations will form the basis for our argument on the parameters of media engagement in Chapter 2, where we present the conceptual building blocks of our understanding of engagement as a nexus of relationships, highlighting the various elements it embodies within public mediated spheres. Later in Part III of the book, we offer two in-depth case studies using the nexus of relations we see within the parameters of media engagement. One case concerns news and family relations in the context of mobile social media news, particularly inter- and intragenerational relations in Southeast Asia during the COVID crisis. Another case concerns the Belarusian protests and political crackdown on citizens, with both mobile social media engagement and 'courtyard' protests by communities offering resources for momentary resistance to authoritarian violence and restrictions on communicative freedom (see Laputsla 2021).

These case studies underscore the contingencies of media engagement. In Chapters 5, 6 and 7, we find configurations of media engagement and disengagement that are highly sensitive to situated contexts and processes. Our case studies move beyond examples of engagement in the Global North in order to offer an analysis of power dynamics, in particular, historical and social vectors of engagement in public and mediated spheres. The regional and temporal specificities of our cases – Belarusian protests in the past year, or Chinese Malay and Vietnamese news audiences during the COVID-19 crisis – are examples of the differential relations of power and resources for local and transnational citizens. Although case studies that are concerned with local patterns of engagement are context sensitive, we hope our analysis of these challenging civic and media experiences highlight both common tendencies and local variations for a critical analysis of the parameters of engagement as nexus of relations that are processual in nature.

Such cases suggest varying tones of media engagement in changing public and mediated spheres. In the concluding Chapter 8, we reflect on affect and intensities of engagement, playing with the metaphor of music, in particular, chordal relations, to explore rhythmic qualities of engagement as cultural resonance, or vibrations (see Henriques et al 2014; Hill 2018). We suggest that there are tonal arrangements for media engagement in our case studies on public knowledge and social movements during the COVID-19 crisis. Various tonal arrangements for media engagement encompass societal conflict, public and commercial media infrastructures, political resistance, at times social resilience, and the dynamics of (dis)engagement and cultures of negation in public and mediated spheres.

TRACING MEDIA ENGAGEMENT

The play-off between engagement as performance metric and subjective experience is a sign of the tensions around the meaning of the term within the media industries and academic research. In recent work on media industries and engagement (see Hill and Steemers 2017; Hill 2018; Evans 2019 amongst others), we find a strategic use of engagement as a performance indicator for economic targets. This is an instrumental meaning of the term, where engagement is something to capture and measure in specific places (platforms, channels, or influencer profiles) and at certain times (hourly, daily, weekly leaderboards). Ratings, social media analytics and newspaper reviews are the primary ways of measuring audience engagement as a basic definition of interest. And yet engagement is so much more than the public's interest in something, as it captures people's subjective positions, such as producers creating content that engages us, professionals promoting and marketing content for mass and niche audiences, and fans, producers and users experiencing media content.

Conceptually, there are porous meanings of the term engagement *with* the media and *via* the media (see also Carpentier 2011). Engagement with the media is often understood as audience-citizen-user involvement with issues concerning the ownership, control and/ or practices of specific media, such as monopoly structures, journalistic values, or editing/nonediting of social media. Our emphasis is on an engagement 'with' that to which the media mediates us – its factual and fictional representations. And it is important to keep in mind that even in regard to factual materials, the media in fact mediate: they provide discursive assemblages of textual/visual/aural elements, never a 'direct contact' with reality. While the conceptual distinction is significant, empirically it is not always easy to separate the two, not least in regard to the experiences of audiences and users themselves. Unless otherwise noted, our discussion will focus on perceptual, cognitive and affective engagement with diverse media texts, artefacts and events.

To add to the messiness of engagement with and via the media, we also point out engagement against the media. A key point we make in this book is that such discourses of media engagement tend to ignore disengagement. To choose not to engage with media is also a regular part of people's daily routines. In some cases, disengagement is a strategy, a deliberate action to turn away from negative content, propaganda, or toxic comments, and to turn towards something else. Negation, then, is just as significant to our understanding of engagement as appreciation. Gray's recent work *Dislike Minded* (2021) identifies the absence of academic attention to dislike, noting how fan dislike, or social media dislike-minded conversations tend to operate in the shadows. Social media interfaces actively obscure dislike-minded thinking, focusing on likes and appreciation. As Gray notes, dislike is relational and critical; how we dislike media tells us about meaning making and displeasure. Whilst Gray's audience research on dislike focuses mainly on popular culture, their sense of dislike as relational chimes with our understanding of (dis)engagement as relational. We address how cultures of negation, be these related to dislike mindedness, or disengagement, and disconnect, can be understood as resources for living – for example, a negation of news in authoritarian societies can be a resource for hope by citizens, especially during a time of the COVID-19 crisis (see Chapter 6).

The industry-based meaning of engagement is not merely a measurement of interest, attention, or consumption. In today's media landscape, the growing power of algorithms shapes our experience of software and platforms, generating content suggestions, nudging behaviour patterns and generically labelling media for our attentive engagement (Bucher 2018). As abundance and speed increase the competition for attention, and as the media environment becomes denser, the odds of getting and holding attention to any message generally decreases – with long-range and as yet not fully understood consequences for not only engagement, but also memory, cognitive skills, self-reflection and more. As we develop personal strategies for navigating the daily tsunami of information, 'infoglut' as Andrejevic (2013) calls it, 'distraction' and 'disengagement' become less the antithesis of attention and more of an attribute: media attention is increasingly characterised by (disjointed) seriality (Jackson 2009). Pettman (2106) argues that the speed of social media also fragments us into ever-smaller micro-zones of attentive engagement, be it fandom or political tribes.

Media attention and engagement are entangled with various empirical and theoretical notions about consumption. Our focus on media engagement sets certain limits on the possible domains of relevance regarding consumption, yet consumption still offers an array of pertinent interfaces. Commercial logics are most obvious: engagement can point to market relations that offer us that which we need to survive and that which we might desire: the promise of satisfaction and pleasure. It is most commonly exemplified by the many forms of advertising, shopping and commercial variants of entertainment, from engaging TV ads to product-pushing online 'influencers'. Consumption intertwines with mediated popular culture, and – even if less obviously so – with politics as well, as work by Micheletti (2003) and Sassatelli (2007) has highlighted. There can be political and ethical motivations for consumption, and a commercial and civic mix intertwined in such modes of engagement.

Whilst work in attention economies, algorithmic logics, and citizen-consumer research are relevant to media industry definitions of engagement, we want to thus move, as we have noted, beyond these meanings that tend to prioritise quantitative data and economic targets towards a sense of engagement as offering sociocultural as well as economic or reputational value. Engagement is, of course, a regular part of people's daily routines, such as watching a live sports event. New and returning audiences-consumers-users are monitored through ratings, appreciation indexes and social media buzz for content now, compared to the previous week, the last month or year. Similar to sports teams who play every season, performance metrics accumulate into a more longitudinal picture of a production company, content, artefact or experience that audiences like or dislike, that consumers will pay for and that users will share and comment on.

Existing engagement models primarily represent audiences, fans and consumers as market value, never more so than within platform economics and the positive values given to attention and appreciation (Jenkins, Green and Ford 2013). Napoli's (2010) discussion of engagement within the media industries highlights six components: attentiveness, loyalty, appreciation, emotion, recall and attitude. These components position engagement within identifiable

quantitative methods, a pragmatic check list for audience information databases in the media, arts and cultural sectors – note how these
components accentuate positive engagement. Criticism of existing
engagement models has focused on audiences' immaterial labour
exploited by global capitalism; the work of audiences and their time,
emotion and amateur production are used to generate economic value,
and, just as important, passion economics, such as fans who form life-
long attachments with a particular brand or celebrity (Arvidsson and
Bonini 2015).

With regard to engagement in the performing arts, the use of the
term audience engagement is mainly viewed as a progressive step in
seeing audiences, fans and consumers as active agents. For example,
Walmsley (2019) charts the absence of audience engagement as a
cultural value, noting how audiences have been represented as ticket
sales rather than people present, listening and reflecting in a theatre;
they argue for audiences as central to artistic exchange within arts
organisations and propose an engagement model for the sector. Such
a point about the active audience has long been part of media, communication and cultural studies, charting back to early work in cultural studies and feminist perspectives on audience engagement – for
example, engaging with soap operas, or early work in fan studies – for
example, intense engagement with an artefact or celebrity.

A recent overview of the use of the term media engagement in film
studies, fan studies and transmedia storytelling by Elizabeth Evans
(2019) is instructive with regard to this point. Various engagement
models for screen media, such as films, television, or gaming, tend
to be hierarchical and temporal, and medium specific. For example,
Plantinga (2018) argues for an ethics of storytelling within film, iden-
tifying the significance of characterisation, or narrative endings, in
cultivating certain thoughts and responses by film spectators. Evans
goes beyond a medium-specific engagement model. They draw on
extensive empirical research of creative producers and audiences in
transmedia storytelling to propose their own model of engagement
that is inherently transmedia – for example, the way fans of a particular transmedia franchise will engage both with specific forms and
across genres and media, from film to comic books to gaming, and
back again. Evans proposes a transmedia model of engagement that
contains four components: behaviour (receptive, or interactive), form

of response (emotional, cognitive, physical), cost (money, time) and value (economic, artistic, reputational). The flexibility of the model is key, as the components work for a specific medium, say film, and across various forms, such as the Marvel universe. Ultimately, Evans is interested in how engagement with transmedia storytelling tells us about different values for engagement and experiences by producers and audiences.

Our interest in experience is at the point where it shapes engagement:

> It is the experiences, both shaping and shaped, which variously precede, inform and then follow media engagements that are often the real matter at issue. Research into media engagement is often, if only partly, an inquiry into the realm of the experiential and its contemporary cultural resources, with all the challenges that implies.
>
> (Corner 2017: 5)

As Corner (2017: 5) has shown, by opening up the meaning of engagement as human experience, we can use the term as a resource for living, a means to improve the conditions for social and cultural equality.

A significant focus on our meaning of engagement concerns itself with problematising power relations and hegemonies – we mobilise currents within cultural theory, critical political economy and critical neoliberalism studies, which emphasise process and context as essential to empirical and theoretical modes of analysis (see Dawes and Lenormand 2020). While the terms in this nexus such as participation, subjectivity and experience are readily coupled with the concept of media engagement, it is necessary to move towards a more nuanced understanding of the core concept when conducting theoretical and empirical research. In our analysis, the theme of affect and emotionality features significantly across synonyms for engagement. Media engagement can never be seen as an exclusively rational/cognitive phenomenon nor, as we shall discuss, can it be reduced to merely the emotional.

The vocabulary of emotions and feelings is slippery and problematic, as Frosh (2011), a psychologist well-versed in social theory, underscores. We use *emotion* and *experience* in a largely descriptive, common-sense way, while we see *affect* as a theoretically more ambitious notion. Media engagement is an emotional experience that can embody, for example, moral passion, resentment, pleasure, curiosity, fear, anxiety, anger, humour and not least identity processes – which in turn relate to the subjectivity of the self, both individual and collective. For Frosh (2011) there are roughly speaking two kinds of experiences: the lived reality of the moment, and our thoughts, feelings and sensory responses within the experience itself; and then the memories of our experience, what stays with us, what we archive and talk about and reflect on after the experience itself. These ways of understanding experience intertwine with each other over time, so this becomes a process of experiencing reality and reflecting on our experience of reality, which sometimes can be in harmony and at other times in conflict with each other.

The more challenging notion of 'affect' has gained prominence in recent years; there has emerged an 'affective turn' in the humanities and social sciences, inspired by Spinoza, among others (see e.g. Massumi 2002; Manning 2010; Gregg and Seigworth 2010). In media studies, Papacharissi (2014) has incorporated and mobilised the term for analyses of social media. She suggests that the term helps us to analyse modes of political engagement that hover beyond formalised expressions of opinion. Moreover, it indicates how unformed and spontaneous political sentiment may accumulate, moving from the latent to the manifest, giving new shape to engagement and participation. In simple terms, if emotion is a 'state' one is in, affect has to do with the dynamics of how one got there.

The significance of affect can be understood if we think of engagement as shaped by something more powerful than just feelings inside the hearts of individuals, namely, shared social experience. Thus, affect brings in the collective side of emotions, and derives from the work of several specific authors, as Papacharissi (2014) describes. One source that she emphasises is Raymond Williams and his notion of 'structures of feeling'. According to Sharma and Tygstrup (2015: 2), the idea of structures of feeling 'compliments the analysis of the social and material infrastructure of reality with a third layer: that of affective infrastructure'. They go on to suggest that affectivity is 'what tinges or colours the way in which we take part in the environments we find ourselves placed into' (2015: 14). For Williams (1977), structures of feeling give expression to prevailing cultural currents and moods of a given historical moment; they are implicit and inchoate, yet can still impact on people's political horizons. Their political character can of course vary greatly; they can unfortunately even manifest unsavoury sentiments (e.g. populism).

Affect can be seen as dynamic, collective emotionality that connects with people's shared social experiences; affect animates engagement and helps motivate participation. Here, the work of Pedwell (2014) on empathy as an affective relation is pertinent to our discussion. Pedwell challenges assumptions of the universality of affect, arguing that there are multiple configurations of empathy relations. In addition, their focus on how empathy is connected with individuals, shared encounters and situated contexts is something we explore in our research on the various modes of affective and cognitive engagement in specific media and societal contexts. Pedwell's emphasis on the transnational, highlighting how empathy is contingent on feelings and emotions that we experience and articulate, in particular, historical, sociopolitical contexts, is certainly something we find in our analysis of how affective engagement works in practice for our case studies of the Belarusian protests, and the affective negation of news in Southeast Asia during the COVID-19 crisis.

Here, the way in which the affective dimensions of engagement are enmeshed with power relations is crucial. It serves to underscore how affective relations offer ways of seeing, feeling and, at times, contesting power. As Anderson notes: 'understanding how power functions in the early 21st century requires that we trace how power operates through affect and how affective life is imbued with relations of power' (2014: 8).

If engagement is seen as a subjective disposition, participation can be treated as observable behaviour, that is, forms of doing. Thus, the subjective state of engagement can be treated as a prerequisite for observable acts of participation (for further discussion, see Dahlgren 2009). Participation, basically, is comprised of forms of social practices. Shove, Pantzar and Watson (2012) theorise practices as consisting of the complex mobilisation, coordination and not least transformation of pertinent elements that include materials (media devices), competences (skills) and social meaning. From this horizon, it is easy to see the role of subjective engagement in foregrounding participation.

It is of course very possible that any given state of engagement does not necessarily result in what would be considered political and cultural participation, or that the actors themselves may deem their engagement as constituting participation (while others, e.g., researchers, may not). While some citizens participate in the media with the aim of altering their policies, regulation and/or financing – via various stakeholder organisations and regulatory bodies – such engagement is a slow and often frustrating investment of energy. Even in regard to the internet, despite the communicative freedom it affords, users remain, in structural terms, subordinate providers of data for the tech giants, with little potential for impact (Zuboff 2019).

In sum, while engagement is largely seen as an affective experience, it always also incorporates some elements associated with the cognitive functions of the mind, such as forms of analysis, calculation, argumentation, and so on. Indeed, the balance and dynamic between the affective and the cognitive will vary, and often provide fruitful analytic insight into the vicissitudes of media engagement (see Corner 2011). For example, interviewees can express their engagement in emotional terms, but they also provide reasons for why they are engaged with a particular media phenomenon (regardless of how we might evaluate the quality of the reasoning). Affect, emotion and reason are always, to varying degrees, co-present and active in human agency, not least concerning engagement.

Liberal democratic theory has long had a problem with emotion and affect, and strived to filter it out, leaving an analytic perspective of purely rational political actors (Hall 2005). This attempt to return to what is at least implicitly a pre-Freudian model of the psyche has proven to be a dead end, both in politics and culture. In the study of political communication and even in the voting process, some scholars have now come to underscore the importance of emotion (see, e.g., Coleman 2013). Ultimately, politics and culture as well as subjectivity itself – straddle the rational-emotional distinction, without safety nets, and engagement can be understood as in part predicated on the tensions between them. Trying to deny one side or the other merely hinders our understanding of human agency

ENGAGEMENT MATTERS

A note of origin, our book started out as a series of conversations at international symposia on media engagement at Lund University in Sweden in 2015 and University of Westminster in the UK in 2016. We had previously written about media and political engagement (Dahlgren 2009, 2013), and audience engagement (Hill 2007, 2015, 2017), and engagement as cultural resonance (2018), and our research came together whilst at these symposia, in the company of participants also working on this theme. For example, the schedule for the Lund symposium started with a discussion of the rational and affective dimensions of media engagement; there was an example of the tonal quality of news and public engagement, a forewarning of the politics of news and 'Brexiternity'. Some scholars analysed the value judgements made about engagement as political, socio-economic and cultural, in the broader framework of media in a digital and commercial age; others situated engagement in comparative studies, tracing engagement patterns for transnational audiences and citizens. Researchers noted how policy discourses and documents referred to public engagement in name only, lacking citizen perspectives and opportunities for civic agency. Academic and industry experts reflected on new currencies of engagement for diversity in public service media, or the digital divide. There was also a timely reminder of assumptions regarding audience engagement as presupposing meaningful encounters with the media; and yet mundane media, digital boredom and disengagement are a routine part of our everyday lives.

The symposium ended with a roundtable discussion, chaired by John Corner. His synthesis and critical reflections on engagement, both in his writings (*Theorising Media* 2011) and at this event, started a shift in the tone and meaning of the word engagement. The symposium was a space for us to deconstruct the term (what is engagement?), reflect on its descriptive properties (it's only a word!) and glimpse its potential for analytical purchase (engagement matters). All the participants at the symposium, in one way or another, unboxed the term engagement. Normally, engagement is the tick in the box on a survey, or the diagram displaying engagement analytics for a digital platform. Policy and industry discourses on engagement tend to use a narrow sense of consumer and public engagement that fits within a particular political economic framework and serve certain powerful actors. Fresh perspectives on media engagement are needed to counterbalance these dominant discourses (see Walvaart et al 2019). A special issue of the journal *Media Industries* (Hill and Steemers 2017) contained various articles on policy and industry engagement, the significance of disengagement, and the identification of new currencies of engagement within academic and industry research.

We hope scholars in particular areas of expertise outside of the remit of this book (e.g. fandom, gaming, sports, arts and theatre, or political communication) will continue the conversation on engagement. To be engaged with the media means more than being taken up with, diverted by, or reactive to a cultural artefact or event. Engaging with the media, in the context of politics, society and culture is a significant psychological investment in something or someone that matters in that moment and/or over a longer period of time. This is why engagement matters; it tells us about the connections across reason and rationality, affect and emotion, and why people connect or disconnect with politics and popular culture.

OUTLINE OF THE BOOK

This book has a threefold structure. Part I on 'Mapping Engagement' starts with this chapter *Understanding Media Engagement*. This introduction explores the key concept of media engagement, charting various terms for the concept, and arguing for a new, tighter analytical notion of the term rooted in an understanding of media, culture and democracy. This introductory chapter has hopefully guided the reader through the definitions and current research on media engagement, arising from advertising, media and communications, political communication, cultural studies and sociology. Our aim has been to outline the broad horizon of research on media engagement before offering our more focused analytical purchase on the concept. It is in this chapter that we have made our strategic intervention into the commercial and industrial definition of media engagement as a pragmatic term for audience attention and audience information systems.

Chapter 2 *Parameters of Media Engagement* outlines the sense of media engagement as a spectrum of phenomena that is protean, that is, ever changing. This spectrum addresses the cognitive and affective modes of engagement of citizens and publics, audiences and users, highlighting the different positions and intensities of engagement in various contexts. Thus, we see engagement as having a spectral character, which includes affective and cognitive modes, switching between positive and negative engagement, and disengagement. From this overarching discussion on our definition of media engagement, we now turn to developing a matrix that can help orient its empirical investigation. Our notion of engagement as a nexus informs the specific parameters of media engagement that we offer. Each parameter seeks to highlight a definitive attribute about media engagement, offering an angle of approach, yet we assume that the parameters work in conjunction with each other. At the same time, in any specific instance of media engagement, some parameters will probably have greater relevance than others and relate to each other in differing configurations. Our parameters are media contexts, motivations, modalities, intensities and consequences. The five parameters of engagement offer empirical ports of entry for researching concrete manifestations of the phenomenon. The fact that the relative salience of each parameter is likely to vary from case to case also alerts us to the importance of being sensitive to context and contingencies in our analyses. Researching media engagement may well involve keeping several balls in the air at the same time, but such arduous conceptual and empirical juggling has the potential to elucidate it in ever new and significant ways

In Part II 'Changing Public Settings for Engagement', Chapter 3 *Vectors of Media Engagement* looks back at the various trajectories of media and political engagement; we trace distinct waves in academic research, from intensive media and political engagement in the 1960s and 1970s, characterised by social movements against social, gender and racial inequality, to a lament about an absence of political engagement in the 1980s and 1990s, characterised by a hyper attention to consumerism and individualism. This timeline takes us into the present day and re-engagement with digital and social media as potentially new paths to the political; at the same time, such re-engagement practices also point to a rise in populism, the production and spread of disinformation and negative social media engagement.

Chapter 4 *Public Spheres and their Contingencies* broadly positions our definition of media engagement within work done on public political spheres, arguing for ways to study the vicissitudes of media engagement. In this chapter, we discuss the significance of civic cultures and cultural citizenship to our thinking on engagement, underlining how we need to pay close attention to the ways these modes of engagement may come together with distinct consequences in public spheres.

In Part III of this book, we offer 'Case Studies in Public Knowledge and Political Engagement', with an in-depth and original analysis of public knowledge and news engagement during the COVID-19 crisis, and political and social activism in Belarus during the global crisis. These case studies hinge on our perspective of engagement as a nexus of relations. We offer a contextual analysis of media and political engagement to highlight how the personal, the sociocultural, and the political all link up in a media engagement that is attentive to specific events and contexts and the subjective power of human experience.

Chapter 5 *Audience Engagement: Researching News in Southeast Asia* offers an empirical example of Southeast Asian news audiences, specifically Chinese-Malay and Vietnamese millennial audiences of mainstream and alternative news across national television and transnational digital news feeds. We draw upon 30 interviews with young audiences using an interview guide specifically designed for parameters of media engagement. News engagement is situated in a specific regional context, during the time of the global pandemic of COVID-19. This chapter offers methodological reflections on designing an audience study for news engagement; and the chapter offers a practical step by step guide to how to design qualitative interviews using the parameters of engagement.

Chapter 6 *News Relations* is an analysis of the news project for Southeast Asia. We find a pervasive culture of negation for news set within a climate of news censorship and avoidance of politics. News engagement is embedded in routines and rituals for intergenerational households; parents watch national television news, or read daily newspapers that are subject to censorship by the government, and younger adults living at home engage with mainstream news, non-mainstream and international news. For this millennial generation, their news information flows through their phones and is deconstructed within private social media groups. It's a form of mobile news, whilst travelling on a train, standing in an elevator, or sitting in a taxi; and this mode of news on the go is funnelled through informal news groups (friends and siblings) in order to further filter, check and verify the news as valid. This type of multidirectional news engagement is shaped by millennial audiences learning to live with the contradictions of media power in Southeast Asia.

Chapter 7 *The Belarus Protests* focuses on media and political engagement, drawing on the developments in Belarus since the much-contested presidential election in August of 2020. The popular (and international) responses to what was perceived as a grossly rigged election triggered a massive mobilisation of Belarus citizens against the authority of the state. This was the immediate context of engagement; the broader context can be found in the aftermath of the collapse of communism in 1989, and more specifically in the rule of President Lukashenko since 1994, known as 'Europe's last dictator'. The frustrations and anger that had built up over the years reached a tipping point with the perceived fraudulent election in August fuelling the motivation. The engagement became intensified with the brutal repression on the part of the police and military. An intense disengagement with state media was counter-pointed with engagement in social media, especially the app Telegram, which has been difficult for the authorities to hack or block. The modality of engagement has been both affective – mobilising collective identity and support for demonstrations and other forms of resistance – as well as cognitive: much strategic information is shared through this app. As of this writing, the consequences are still unclear; the situation remains tense and unresolved.

We conclude the book with Chapter 8 *Contingencies of Media Engagement* and our reflections on the case studies of public knowledge and political engagement as a means to think through power relations. Our argument about the parameters of media engagement draws upon various scholarly research within political and social theory, media and cultural studies, which sees engagement 'within a larger range of psychological orientations to the world and to the artefacts within it' (Corner 2017: 4). We turn to the metaphor of sound and chordal relations to understand how all the five parameters of media engagement work together, each parameter makes a particular sound, and together they create a certain tonal arrangement – for example, the sound of despair for news in authoritarian societies during the COVID-19 crisis. Above all, we emphasise how our generative theory of media engagement as a nexus of relations is something we hope researchers can use to think through further contingencies for the changing public settings of media engagement and what this means for audiences and citizens in the context of their lives.

2

PARAMETERS OF MEDIA ENGAGEMENT

INTRODUCTION

We argue that media engagement is best understood as a spectrum of phenomena that is processual and protean; it is a shape-changer. We cannot grasp it theoretically or empirically as a simple on-off phenomenon; even disengagement has its dynamics and variegated aspects. Media engagement is situated in ever-evolving circumstances; we should expect tensions and even contradictions in its dynamics. Our notion links the personal, the sociocultural, and the political, and these elements serve as a horizon in our understanding. This horizon embodies a spectrum of parameters (see Figure 2.1): these address the cognitive and affective modes of engagement of citizens and publics, audiences and users, highlighting the different positions and intensities of engagement in various contexts.

Our analyses of engagement as a spectrum of phenomena seek to illuminate the myriad ways people engage and disengage with the media, and how this differs from person to person, or group to group, across vectors of political and cultural engagement. This enables us to grasp the value and meaning of engagement as something played out in the concrete contexts of political and cultural institutions, and

DOI: 10.4324/9781003179481-3

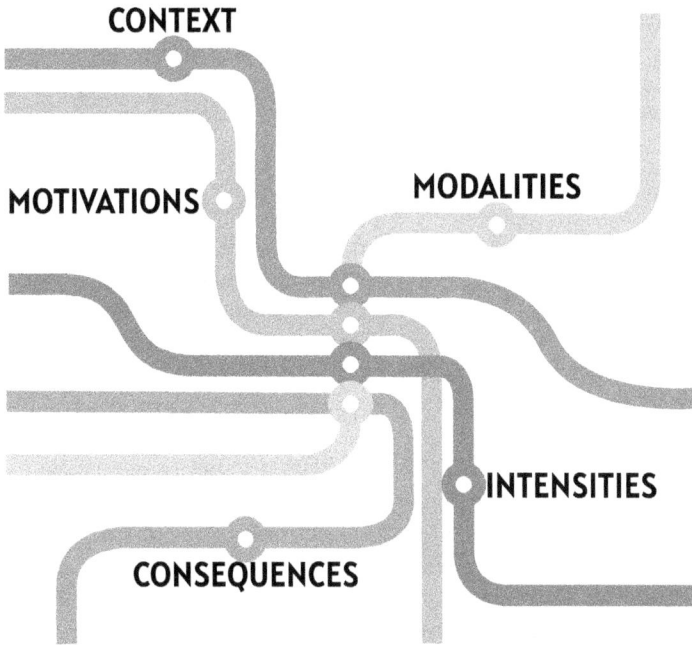

CONTEXT

MOTIVATIONS

MODALITIES

INTENSITIES

CONSEQUENCES

Figure 2.1 'Parameters' graphic illustration by J.C. Lee

media and creative industries. If we thus conceptualise media engagement as a horizon composed of specific parameters, these parameters can serve as analytic ports of entry that facilitate an empirical analysis in any given case. Overall, our aim is to highlight how engagement is a useful concept for thinking through our relations with media as contextual, processual and relational.

FIVE PARAMETERS

Our notion of engagement as a spectrum thus informs the specific parameters of media engagement that we offer below. Each parameter seeks to highlight a definitive attribute about media engagement, offering an angle of approach, yet we assume that the parameters work in conjunction with each other. At the same time, in any specific instance of media engagement, some parameters will undoubtedly have greater relevance than others and relate to each other in differing configurations. Our parameters are contexts, motivations, modalities, intensities and consequences.

Contexts

Context looms large among our parameters. This parameter points to the major factors that serve to situate and delimit any specific case of media engagement. These factors can be – and often are – on the large, societal level, taking a variety of forms: cultural, political, economic and (socio-)psychological. Moreover, they can be material, as in the case of an economic crisis, or ideational, as with a particular political climate. Relevant features of the media landscape itself of course will also in some way define the context, not least as disseminators of various discourses – dominant, hegemonic discourses as well as counter-hegemonic ones. Prevailing hegemonic discourses can play a decisive role in shaping context – thereby impacting on media engagement. In our view, the most compelling overarching analytic frame in this regard is the critique of neoliberalism, that is, the prevalent view that places market forces and commercial logic in the driver's seat of societal development, sidelining democratic accountability and concerns for the common good.

We mentioned neoliberalism in Chapter 1; what we underscore is that this fundamentalist, deregulated incarnation of modern capitalism erodes democracy and engenders social inequality and devastation. Emerging gradually as a vision between the world wars, it became firmly embodied in policies in the West during the 1980s (see Peck 2010; Harvey 2007, for insightful histories). Neoliberalism is not just economic policy, it is also a mindset, the 'spirit of our age' (Clapp 2021). The marketisation of most personal values and social practices has profound bearing on all facets of the social world, including democracy (Brown 2015), the media (Meyers 2019) and cultural policy (McGuigan 2016). Today, neoliberalism reaches not just globally but also into the micro-meshes of everyday life, impacting on our identities and subjectivity in evermore subtle ways (Bröckling 2016). It is embodied in hegemonic discourses, but it is also marked by contradiction and counter-hegemonies, rather than comprising a secure, stable system.

As the contemporary historical phase of capitalism, neoliberalism is processual and variegated (Dawes and Lenormand 2020) – like media engagement itself. There are local variations in its manifestations – it can be incorporated into autocratic and illiberal systems as well as traditional democratic ones. Analyses must be alert to differences as well as basic similarities: local heterogeneity exists alongside global homogeneity. Thus, elucidating the lines of impact of this meta-context requires detailed analysis, and involves critical reflection on (often less visible) power relations; the notion of 'the political' – that collective conflicts of interest can potentially arise in any societal context – remains ever potentially relevant.

Following from these broader societal horizons, the media landscape is, of course, always a pertinent contextual feature: their institutional structures, technical aspects, accessibility, usage and/ or content. We can distinguish, on the one hand, between formal media institutions, with their economies and recognised distribution pathways, such as public service media, and official websites for news, along with the regional and global distribution and flow of content. On the other hand, we have informal media economies and piracy pathways, such as virtual private networks (VPNs), with friendly sharing of clouds and passwords having become increasingly relevant. This includes websites with the latest films and TV shows on offer without windowing or regional barriers (see Lobato and Thomas 2015). And perhaps most central – at least for many people and groups, of course is an over-expanding universe of the internet, in particular, social media. This can easily become the joker in the deck, given the ubiquity of social media and the difficulty in obtaining precise pictures of use, content and flow, but tools for big data analysis have made these aspects of media context more amenable for mapping. And in many cases, it can be the simple restrictions and closures of the internet and social media that are the most analytically compelling in contextual terms.

Details about audiences and users also come into play in illuminating context, for example, access, attention factors, pre-existing knowledge, skills and practices in regard to relevant genres, platforms and their logics. Further, the place and time of media engagement are significant. There is the location of a media production, such as a studio or outside event for television news, or the private home of an internet celebrity and their daily vlogs. The place in which we engage with content is also significant, including the physical space of our home, or our seat on the train from work, and also the region we live in and our access and social context to engagement. Such attention to the contexts of media engagement allows for transnational media and audiences, where local, regional and global contexts impact on the ways people engage and disengage with media in the spheres of politics and popular culture.

Media contexts thus include features at both the sites of production and reception in local, national and transnational settings; today's complex and ever-evolving media landscape, not least in the online world, requires careful attention to understand how specific contexts impact on engagement. The time of media engagement matters, whether engagement is occurring with live news coverage, or a current social protest, or through catchup services and archival content on streaming platforms. The context of time connects with intensities in the parameters of media engagement.

Finally, we must also take into account what might be termed 'epistemic contexts' – contingencies concerning what and how we know about the world. Here we highlight 'post-truth', which we discussed in the previous chapter. Largely linked to radical right-wing politics, this term underscores how affective messages can sideline factual information; this is a significant epistemic context in public spheres today. Likewise, all the trolling, disinformation, propaganda, hate and threats now rampant on the internet serve to redefine the online environment into a different context than it was at at its launching in the mid-1990s. Epistemic contexts ultimately connect with, enhance or impede the hegemonic discourses that reside at the broader societal level.

It may seem that societal contexts can generate an infinite inventory of possible factors to manage, but, in fact, in any given situation, not all will be of relevance. In most cases, it will soon become quite clear which ones will be useful in shedding analytic light; one can then proceed to probe them in depth. With the context established, one can then turn to the other parameters to flush out their dynamics and see how their total interrelation generates media engagement.

Motivations

This refers to the intentionality behind the engagement. All human action has some sort of intentionality behind it, even if this resides at an unconscious level. The subjective predispositions behind and/or evoked by engagement offer another significant parameter of analysis. Elucidating motivation need not be psychologistic or reductionist in its approach, but can rather search for patterns of perceptions and values that are socially situated and specific to various categories of actors. Unravelling them from each other and tracking down their social origins may at times be a challenge, but the effort can tell us important things about the media engagement.

Analyses of the motivations behind media engagement take into account interest, from basic, everyday curiosity to a concerted and rational drive for knowledge (Dahlgren 2013). Motivations leading people to the same media content can of course vary; for example, the motivations for engaging with a documentary about memory and genocide may arise from an interest in human rights, or a drive for better understanding of trauma, or information on amnesty. The motivations to engage with such a documentary shape the modalities of engagement (see below) with such a genre, both in terms of how the filmmakers 'address' audiences and how audiences actually engage with documentary (Hill et al 2019). Other motivations behind engagement can take into account pleasure, such as relaxation, escapism, romance or eroticism, which draws upon affect and emotionality. For example, the motivations for engaging with crime drama may arise from an interest in the genre, a particular writer or performer, and a love of solving the puzzle of crime, thus connecting the genre and storytelling with a prior knowledge of and interest in this kind of drama experience (Turnbull 2014).

Another motivation relates to socialities that tell us something about the ways we are members of various communities, groups and networks. This can connect the reasons for engaging with factuality or fictionality in television content, for example, with peer recommendations, or a sense of belonging in fan communities. Two further motivations include efficacy, relating to a confidence in one's ability and a sense that engagement can be successfully enacted. First, for example, in relation to political comedy, research suggests that audiences need to feel confident in their ability to understand real-world politics in order to get the humour, interlinking the motivation to engage with a prerequisite of news and genre knowledge for satire (see Doona 2018).

Further, there can also be a sense of duty, where motivation has to do with a feeling of obligation or solidarity, some kind of social value that resides beyond the self. For example, with regard to news, citizens feel a duty to engage with real-world events, but at the same time may feel a lack of efficacy in judging what news they can trust to present facts in ways they can understand. Thus, empirically we would try to illuminate how constraints and opportunities impact on each of these subjective grounds of engagement. Certainly, elucidating the motivations of citizens and audiences will enable an understanding of where engagement is coming from (e.g. industry, genre, narrative, settings) and where it may have an impact on our lived realities (e.g. politics, society, communities of viewers).

Modalities

This points to the communicative character of that on which the engagement builds. One can foresee a rather extensive list of modalities, but it can often be useful to make a simplistic duality of what is in fact a complex amalgam: referring to the discussion above, we can consider affective and cognitive modalities of engagement. An affective modality of engagement builds upon the affective structures within a genre, a particular narrative, or a live event, where through the crafting of engagement we are invited to engage with subjective and emotional issues, personae and characters, or moral dilemmas. Thus, the mood of a live experience will impact on the affective modality of engagement of the crowd; for a memorial, the crowd may feel sad and be moved to tears; for a political rally, the crowd may feel outrage and be moved by anger. Affective engagement is used to great effect in storytelling, inviting a range of emotions, from love, to hate, to indifference, with characters and settings.

Cognitive engagement is a modality that invites more critical thinking, perhaps drawing on the knowledge of citizens to cognitively engage with a political issue, or to ask tough questions of a politician and their claims with regard to the environment, say, or public education. Thus, a cognitive modality of engagement can be crafted by producers to invite citizens and audiences to think through the media about a variety of social, political and moral issues, or to understand more about a particular problem, reflect on the implications of the problem and to potentially do something about it. Affective and cognitive modalities of engagement are often intertwined, increasingly so with the use of artificial intelligence in digital media. They work together in people's experiences of media, at times with a clear invitation to engage with the head and/or the heart, at other times in ambiguous ways that mix these modes of engagement, generating a challenging, or ambivalent, media experience. We return to the affective-cognitive couplet in Chapter 4 in our discussion of public spheres.

Modality is often related to form, such as genres, style and themes, visual and sound engagement, or physical and sensory engagement. Ways of engaging with fictional genres, like comedy or melodrama, will shape our overall experience, drawing on genre knowledge about characters and storylines, relying on skills with regard to character identification – for example, typical narrative tropes, or transmedia storyworlds (Evans 2019). Engaging with news, or documentary, relies on a different set of skills and genre knowledge, including referential integrity, assessing truth claims and assessing factual evidence. Genre, then, is a key mode of engagement for much media content. We only have to look at mixed genres to understand how vital this is to shifting modalities of engagement; what is fake news and how ought we to affectively and cognitively engage with it?

For certain texts and artefacts, sound engagement will be vital, such as Autonomous Sensory Meridian Response (ASMR), e.g. YouTube videos where soft sounds like whispering or tapping invite sensory modes of engagement. Other texts and artefacts draw on the primacy of the visual, asking us to read visual representations, such as the use of colour and national flags in a political campaign. We ought to be alert to the mixing of sound and visual engagement in the affective structures of content and the cognitive skills we apply to reading the visual and listening to the sound. The way content moves us also includes our physical reactions, and a vital modality of engagement is that of the physical body, including the physicality of performances, the tactile ways stories are told, and the physical responses of people when engaging with the media (see Hill 2018 for further research on audience engagement and genre).

Thus, we have genre-based modalities of engagement, including varying styles in fiction and factuality, with a multitude of themes, and we also have multi-medial, visual, aural, textual variants within and across these forms. The truly interesting cases will of course be those that use mixed forms and mixed modalities of engagement, and will require further empirical and theoretic development. The cognitive and affective dimensions that are embedded in text, or text plus sound, or text plus other visuals, plus sound and movement, and so on, may not be easily ascertained, but even if we may not fully disentangle the various modes of media engagement, our efforts can nonetheless be illuminating. Indeed, being attuned to mixed modes of engagement is perhaps one of the biggest challenges in researching media experiences and raises issues about multi-site and multi-methods for media and cultural studies.

Intensities

Intensity has of course to do with emotional force, but it is also manifested in duration. How long the particular experience of engagement is sustained is of considerable significance, yet this aspect is often ignored. Intensities of engagement lead us to consider what John Corner calls *stages* (2011, 2017) of engagement, modelled with a continuum, subjective dimensions and time scales. This comprises both subjective elements of experience, as well as observable factors of usage and involvement. Stages can be conceived in terms of short-form engagement, the kind of fleeting engagement that can happen for bite-sized content, paratexts and ephemeral media. For example, short, intense periods of binge-watching crime drama can happen during a moment in one's life, perhaps during the break-up of a relationship, an illness and rehabilitation, and then it can be over. We can characterise this as an intense engagement with a genre and cultural artefact, an energising force in everyday life that can become part of the life histories of an individual or collective group of fans.

There are also more sustained ways of engaging with media, where there are deeper connections that involve embedding particular media experiences into the spaces and places of regular routines, family rituals and cultural memories. This kind of intense engagement can occur over a longer period of time, an embedded engagement in the life course of an individual or collective group (Hill 2018). For example, football supporters can remain loyal in their engagement with a team over the course of their lifetime; this is an embedded engagement that becomes part of the identity and everyday practices of an individual or collective group of supporters for a long duration, sometimes passed on within families to future generations. Indeed, our time bonds with media are vital to engagement, impacting on the duration and affective dimensions of engagement.

Some of the most intense experiences we have with media are in the past, embedded in our memory and linked to what Keightley and Pickering (2012) call the mnemonic imagination. For example, the fact that the comedy series *Friends* is the most watched series on Netflix tells us something about the significance of archival content on streaming services, the time we give for watching this comedy in our daily lives, and the time period of the comedy in the 1990s, tapping into trends in nostalgia, and the bond we form with the show, curled up on the sofa for a date with the convivial world of *Friends*. In other cases, the intensity of our engagement with media as connected to memory cultures is a site of contestation. For example, the creative production of drama documentaries can offer a performance of remembering that challenges official state-sanctioned histories, or calls for social justice and greater transparency in the criminal justice system, such as the *Chernobyl* (2019 HBO) series on HBO and related podcast, or *When They See Us* (2019 Netflix) and the related Oprah Winfrey televised special on Netflix. We can see how intensities of engagement are strongly connected to temporal relations with media and memory cultures.

Consequences

This points to the upshot and implications of the particular instance of engagement. Clearly, consequences will be specific to relevant groups, for example, engaged citizens, TV series viewers, media industry actors, and so on. Further, consequences may or may not relate to possible pre-existing goals of engagement; consequences may often be unforeseen and unintentional, especially in regard to broad societal contexts. Also, analyses must take into account the dimension of explicit agency manifested on the part of those who have become engaged. The consequences of engagement can take many forms – from a sense of empowerment, to the experience of pleasure, to the attainment of satisfactory audience statistics for media organisations. We are aware that the consequences to engagement are not necessarily positive; the spread of anti-vaxxer propaganda on social media during the COVID-19 pandemic is but one obvious illustration.

As Corner (2017: 5) notes,

> dis-engagement has been seen for some time as a prevalent social problem ... and there are many forms of engagement with the media of which we can say with confidence that no engagement would have been far better and the web is increasing the number of possible examples here.

There are urgent reasons in the current media landscape for analysing both positive and negative engagement (as well as at times reflecting on the grounds on which we make this distinction), and what we perceive as the intentional and unintentional consequences of political and cultural engagement.

Overall, the five parameters offer ways of thinking through the relations across various vectors of engagement in public and popular spheres. The metaphor of music helps us to see the parameters as connected together; each parameter makes a particular note but together they create a tonal arrangement. We can imagine the way the five parameters are chordal relations.[1] Just as you can hear a musical arrangement for the piano, made up of chords that relate together to create an overall sound, so too you can hear the parameters relate together as an overall tone, or affective and cognitive arrangement. Such a metaphor enables us to be attentive to affective connections (Pedwell 2014). It's a form of energetic patterning that Henriques et al (2014) speak of in their discussion of affect, rhythm and vibrations in cultural studies. Our interest is in using the five parameters to draw attention to the possibilities of tonal qualities to media engagement, something we return to in our reflections in the conclusion to the book in Chapter 8.

THE CASE OF POPULISM AND PROFESSIONAL WRESTLING

In this section, we offer a brief analysis of populism in professional wrestling in order to address the five parameters of media engagement across political and cultural spheres. In Part III of the book, we consider two further cases in depth, including the case study of news audiences in Southeast Asia, specifically how millennial audiences turn to family and friends to verify and share news, and to question and negate news, during the context of the global pandemic and health crisis of COVID-19. The other case study provides an in-depth analysis of the Belarus protests and the ways in which citizens engaged with social media and 'courtyard' public protests in the context of political power during the COVID-19 pandemic.

In this example, we consider how professional wrestlers shape the affective structure of a live match through a spectrum of engagement that invites their audiences and fans to passionately engage in positive and negative ways with contemporary political culture and the rise of populism in Europe. Here, the sense of engagement as a nexus of relations is vital to understanding the connections between the political context of populism and the cultural context of professional wrestling; we will see how certain weight can be given to particular parameters of engagement, with strong ties for context, modalities and intensities of engagement that shape the motivations and consequences of engagement. This has implications for how we analyse this case as a means of seeing the energising internal force of engagement in the moment of a live media event, a raw and powerful modality in popular culture that is a counterweight to real-world political participation and the contexts of neoliberalism.

POPULIST TENSIONS

'Populism' is a complex and contested concept, and it is sometimes used more in a pejorative rather than analytic manner. Though a difficult signifier to stabilise, it has become pervasive in today's political world. In principle, populism can be politically on the left or the right, but in today's Europe, it is largely right-wing populism that is robustly on the march, often with an extremist profile. (Our view in general aligns itself with the works of authors such as Mudde and Kaltwasser [2017]; Müller [2016]; Urbinati [2019]. In particular, we find Canovan's [1981] emphasis on the notion of 'the people' to be a useful anchoring.)

Canovan (1981) reminds us of a built-in force-field at the core of liberal democracy, two strands that are basically incompatible with each other yet also mutually entangled, complementing each other in convoluted ways. In simplified terms, on the one side, there is an agenda that insists on popular sovereignty, 'power to the people' and government by, for and of the people. Confronting that is the other strand, that of liberal constitutionalism. Traditionally, it has sought, via complicated institutions, laws, and practices, to maintain safeguards, checks and balances in the democratic system. At the same time, it has served to maintain power elites and to modify the direct political impact of 'the people' through various mechanisms of exclusion. These practices inevitably foster social resentment, which can – and at times does – turn political.

Populists fail to appreciate the necessity for constitutional limits on direct democracy. At the same time, they often (and with justification) react against seemingly impenetrable and unresponsive institutions and entrenched hierarchy. The constitutionalists, on the other hand, often fail to reflect on where the grounds of their authority ultimately derive from – that is, 'the people', or more accurately, segments of it – are often dismissed precisely as 'populist'.

Much of this is being played out in the current neoliberal context, and the rise of populism must be seen in part as a response to liberal democracy's failure to deliver on its societal vision. Thus, populists will claim that they represent 'the people' – appealing often to a sense of collective identity perceived to be under threat – while in fact they usually only have the support of a fraction. Moreover, they veer towards authoritarianism, and generally reject pluralism, often in xenophobic and racist terms – thereby excluding many from their notion of 'the people'. Constitutionalists – usually embodied in the political, economic and legal elites, and mainstream media – claim that the prevailing order is the best arrangement for 'the people'. Yet at the same time, this order is also serving to deepen social divisions and deprivations. We need to keep this tension in mind, and avoid reductionist views such as 'liberal' (good) versus 'populist' (bad).

CARNIVALESQUE WRESTLING

As Castleberry et al (2019) note, professional wrestling can invert real-world issues, using the carnivalesque to process the political in athletic performances. The research in this section explores wrestling and European politics, drawing on qualitative semi-structured interviews with professional wrestlers, videos of matches and participant observations of live matches. In particular, the example of Marcus Shilling's performance as Marcus of Man, with a Brexit storyline, exemplifies the spectrum of engagement where an explicitly political storyline is used to deliberately invite intense negative engagement from the live audience towards a right-wing political persona.

Shilling is a British citizen who has made his home in Sweden. He joined Stockholm Wrestling (STHLM) and, working with the company, created a 'stereotypical English character, arrogant with no redeemable qualities' (Shilling 2018). Marcus of Man is a persona based on his homeland of the Isle of Man and channelling the conventional traits of an upper-class politician: elitist, egotistical, right wing, pro-royalty and power hungry. He is also very vain about his hair, a sign of his strength and weakness, referencing both classical mythology (think of Samson whose great physical strength was connected to his long hair) and celebrity politicians (think of the former American President Donald Trump or the British Prime Minister Boris Johnson and their distinctive hairstyles). The context and motivations of engagement mix the professional wrestling industry and its commercial considerations with the character development of Marcus of Man, a villain who allows this professional wrestler to perform the part of a heel.

The context, and indeed meta-context, of engagement provides the real-world backdrop to the character, and its broader storyline, thus shaping the modes of engagement from the live crowds. In terms of the meta-context of neoliberalism and European politics, Shilling and other professional wrestlers used the backdrop of rhetoric regarding free movement for migrants to shape the storytelling. The specific political context of the referendum in which Britain voted to leave the European Union (EU) became a rich narrative vein for his character: 'when Brexit happened I thought I could run with that all the way' (Shilling 2018). As a former Celtic community and Viking stronghold, the Isle of Man is a self-governing crown dependency, similar to the island of Jersey. Although not part of the EU or the United Kingdom, its inhabitants are British citizens with limited rights. They – as a particular category of 'the people' – could not vote in the referendum and yet have been caught up in the outcome. Shilling incorporated the Brexit campaign into his performance: 'I get the crowd to chant Brexit! Brexit! I have a chair with "Hard Brexit" written on it. I have this move called Breakneck Brexit' (Shilling 2018). In such a way, Shilling channels his own feelings of political disempowerment, using his lack of voice in one political setting as a narrative strategy for recognising power inequality and social injustice in a more overtly theatrical setting. For the audience, this interfaces with their motivations – these have obviously to do with pleasure, but also their political inclinations and even possible anger at the political contexts of Brexit and the rise of populism in Europe.

The live context and the theatrical space of the wrestling ring are vital. The live experience ensures a visceral and intense engagement from the crowd, one where physicality and spectacle are part of the event. The modality of affect is clearly overwhelming. Yet this also connects with politics and the news, where what is happening in British and Swedish politics is incorporated into the live performances. Shilling plays this heel in tandem with other wrestlers who also perform characters in the fictional populist party 'Partiet'. With their menacing moves, dark blue arm bands (a conscious colour choice) and grab for power, their political drama parodies the right-wing Swedish Democrats who have been gaining votes and power in Sweden over the past few years. In the recent general election in the autumn of 2018, there was a deadlock in the number of votes, which has resulted in an uncertain future, with various factions refusing to work together, or join forces against this extreme right-wing party. STHLM Wrestling staged a live event around the time of the election with Partiet as a running element of the storyline during the evening.

Clearly, the parallel contexts of the spectacle of the political in the ring, and the Brexit referendum, or the general election in Sweden, taking place at a similar moment in time operate as a stark contrast, creating a form of cultural engagement that is different from the political reality of its live audience. The persona of Marcus of Man is explicitly political, and his fans love to hate him. Shilling spends time on the details of his character – his physical appearance, the way he enters the ring and speaks to the crowd and so on – in order to build up negative emotional engagement. Here we see that the modalities and forms of engagement are vital to this political storyline in professional wrestling. He wants his fans to feel outraged at the abuse of power. He achieves this outcome with verbal cues and physical props: 'I refuse to speak Swedish. When I come out I look very arrogant, looking down at people, literally I look down my nose' (Shilling 2018). The theatrical elements of his engagement profile are centre stage: 'One time I sang my national anthem from the Isle of Man, I just took the microphone and started singing the anthem out of tune and it got a wonderful cacophony of boos from the audience' (Shilling 2018).

Note how the performance, singing, acting and physicality mix together in this characterisation of Marcus of Man. Such performance styles invite mixed modes of engagement, where affective engagement and an intensity of passionate energy shape the live experience. The basic form of the event – professional wrestling, with its (often comic and satirical) dramaturgy and caricatured roles of the antagonists – prefigures much of the engagement, while Marcus of Man and his audience add the particular political dimensions that distinguish his and the audience's performance and add to the overall intensity of the live experience.

The Breakneck Brexit storyline includes an understanding of the parameters of engagement where the context of politics and popular culture shape the modes and intensities of audience engagement:

> I know the crowd at the live matches in Stockholm are intelligent, liberal, in the mid-20s and 30s. It works well with them, they want to be in on the joke, they have more hate in them since Brexit. I push their buttons, play on fears of losing their Swedish identity, being influenced by Britain or America.
>
> (Shilling 2018)

Shilling knows how to generate such negative engagement from the crowd as fuel for his character and other wrestlers in the ring. It is clear to Shilling that his performance is part of a 'visual representation of political culture' (2018). He explains: 'If I am holding someone down or choking someone it can be a metaphor for choking out smaller countries or disempowering people, it can be a visual representation of political reality' (Shilling 2018).

With a character such as Marcus of Man, and the Partiet political storyline, nationalism and xenophobia are used to trigger intense negative engagement with populism. His persona channels the exaggerated rhetoric of right-wing politicians. He makes unfounded claims, spouts untruths about the benefits of breaking with the European Union and effects a politics of blame on migrants, or socialism, for the decline of Great Britain. His representation of populism embraces the more absurd or surreal elements of political culture. Marcus of Man is a ridiculous character. His ego and arrogance crowd the ring, taking all the performance space, grabbing the microphone from the MC (Master of Ceremonies) to shout the loudest and making a show of forcing his political opinions to be heard. By using the symbolic power of political comedy, Shilling presents his character as an object for ridicule. Marcus of Man is a despicable persona, whose performance demonstrates that populist rhetoric and right-wing politicians ought to be exposed and liberal democratic values defended in the current-charged environment.

In this, the parallel between the UK and Sweden is made visible in the form of a British-identified political persona in the fictional Partiet as a warning of what can happen when populism is given power and voice in democratic processes. Shilling's performance of Breakneck Brexit exploits and critiques the way the referendum to remain or leave the European Union has led to political mess and a crisis in British politics and society with long-term repercussions. What is also made visible is that Swedish socialism faces a similar threat from extreme right-wing groups who at present are denied recognition in national governance. As played out in the wrestlers' arena, the Partiet storyline shows how right-wing personas can be overcome, a visual representation of the choking out of populism, with the stark reminder that this is not the case in political reality.

Thus, we see the various consequences of engagement for this case. There is of course the explicit consequences for returning fans and audiences, where the long-running political storyline of Marcus of Man and Partiet is a soap opera, which has cliff-hangers that draw crowds back for more, thus ensuring engagement over a period of time and one that has commercial impact for the event company and the professionals in the ring. There is no explicit outcome of political engagement; this is a theatrical spectacle after all. However, there are implicit consequences that suggest broader social issues and spaces for reflection on political culture. Former wrestler and event manager Dan Ahtola (2018) notes: 'politics is moving closer to wrestling' in its spectacle of excess, the focus on emotions and the way politicians play assigned roles in seemingly intractable conflicts. In such a political environment, the affective climate of live professional wrestling offers a space for political expression: 'you are venting all the disappointment and anger. Everyone is frustrated, everyone is stressed, everyone is disappointed' (Ahtola 2018). As Ahtola (2018) notes, with a clear engagement profile 'everyone knows what to do, you can express strong emotions that you are not allowed to do in everyday life. You don't have to think, you know what to do'. Whilst modern-day politics is messy and full of conflicting emotions and opinions, the power of professional wrestling is that its theatricality and physicality work in ways that (at least potentially) serve to channel negative emotions and transform them into positive experiences. According to Ahtola (2018), anger is not a form of expression that is encouraged in Swedish social life:

> Where can you go and scream in anger? You focus anger in this direction. It is better to be angry than miserable, miserable stays inside you, anger you vent. I think you can act, as an audience you play a part and get into character. When you express yourself you show who you are.

In this case, liberal democracy triumphs: 'The difference is that in wrestling the bad guy is always beaten. You create a conflict and then actually solve it. You win because you are in the right. This is something we do not see in politics' (Ahtola 2018).

A NOTE ON CRITICAL MEDIA RESEARCH

A final note on what we might call the logics or intent on the parameters of media engagement. We have said that media engagement is always potentially the site of power relations in some form or other – the political is an ever-present possibility, although this often may not be visible at first glance. In analytically approaching power relations, we usually – though not de facto – find ourselves on the terrain of critical research.

We use the concept 'critical' in the sense of reflection on relations of power that are problematic or even illegitimate with regard to democratic or humanistic values (for an overview discussion of critical media research see Dahlgren 2013, ch. 7). The first efforts in critical media research, dating from the early 1970s, were largely Marxian in character, but soon other currents emerged, such as feminism, and critical studies in race, post-colonialism, environmentalism and queer studies. The critical tradition today is thus very broad (Keucheyan 2013). In examining power relations and structures, one must keep in focus not only obvious institutional manifestations such as the state, with its legal system, military and police, or the corporate sector, but also cultural and discursive forms, that is, patterns of representation and expression in symbolic environments – which largely means the media.

The media constitute sites where discursive power struggles take place, where hegemony is both manifested and challenged. The concept of hegemony points to prevailing sets of ideas, values and perceptions in society that generate consent and compliance. Hegemonic ideas are usually operative within specific social domains: economics, gender relations, education, employment, reproduction and so forth. Yet there are often discursive linkages between these domains, resulting in a more overarching hegemonic character. Some ideas, to the extent they are hegemonic, are certainly to be lauded for this status – for example, justice, equality, tolerance. Others merit critical confrontation, for example, neoliberalism.

The power of hegemonic ideas is never fully secure; they can be confronted by counter-hegemonic ones. Indeed, power involves not just 'power over', in the form of coercion, constraint, or influence, but also 'power to', that is, enabled political activity – even if the balance is often highly unequal. Further, discursive power in public spheres, especially in regard to political contestation on the internet and social media, may be difficult to pinpoint e.g. which sets of ideas actually have the upper hand (the sprawling 'culture wars'). Alternatively, it may be the case that societal divisions have led to certain ideas having primacy only within specific groups; contestation becomes more cacophonous as conflicting parties share less and less common ground.

Today's critical media research emphasises the links between power and an array of concerns such as meaning, identity and practices, and what these dimensions can reveal about how and why people engage and disengage with media and with politics. Critical media research can shed light on the vitality and vulnerability of civic cultures in specific settings. However, the 'critical' is mostly not built into the actual methods as such, but becomes activated by how the methods are put to use, that is, by the theoretical and conceptual tools that one brings to bear. For example, discourse analysis, help us ask questions about media texts, but critical inquiry about power in those texts will be best facilitated by relevant intellectual tools from the critical tradition.

There is obviously no cookbook for how to best approach the parameters of media engagement with critical research. Each case requires rigorous and imaginative empirical analysis as well as theoretic framing. Keeping in mind what we have said about media engagement – that it should be understood as a spectrum, as protean and as relational – suggests we need to be open and imaginative in our efforts. But we should not be intimidated, and we have much to gain. And while there are no cookbooks, we can glean inspiration from a variety of sources that address critical media research; among recent publications, see, for example, Kackman and Kearney (2018), Ott and Mack (2020), and Croucher and Cronn-Mills (2022).

We note that critical perspectives do not per se have any 'privileged' or guaranteed claim to the truth. Critical research, like all human endeavours, is situated and contingent, so it must therefore at times engage in self-reflection to ensure, as best as possible, that its conceptual tools, data and analyses are of good quality. All human knowledge has its limitations, as Kant so strongly argued; self-critique must thus be a part of the critical methodology (for discussions on this theme, see Felski 2015; Fassin and Harcourt 2019).

CONCLUSION

The five parameters of engagement mapped here are a means to highlight engagement as a nexus of relations, offering empirical ports of entry for researching concrete manifestations of the phenomenon. In analysing the parameters of media engagement, there are no privileged 'methods' that can lead to guaranteed analytic success. Rather, as the above discussion and the example indicate, what is required in the first instance is considerable reflection about the concrete case in question: its apparent empirical elements, its various interlinked and even contradictory relations with other relevant societal phenomena or processes. Procedurally, we suggest dealing with the parameters in the order they are represented here. Certainly, delineating as much as possible about the general context, with its overarching political, social, cultural and/or economic elements, will be a big achievement. Then, mapping the media context will bring the focus down to where engagement will usually become clearly visible. Having the general and media-related contexts in place will in most cases provide rich clues to assist in probing the other parameters.

Motivations, modalities and intensities have to do with human agency and subjectivity, and these are framed by the contexts: glimmerings of what are people doing, desiring, feeling, hoping for, avoiding, afraid of and so on should begin to come into view. Connections to everyday life, to community, to political issues, to identity themes and so on will further fuel the analysis – and hopefully reveal lines of mutual reciprocity between the parameters. Media-related analytic concepts such as genre, factual/fictive, access, control, ritual and so on should serve to put the engagement in conspicuous relief. Consequences may not always be readily accessible: one may be researching an ongoing situation, and only the passage of time will reveal the outcome. Yet often there will be some evidence as to what the media engagement has meant (and for whom), what it upholds or changes, or what it may lead to. In the concluding Chapter 8, we reflect on the meaning of engagement as resonance, for example, the way engagement, as an energising internal force, can reverberate in changing public and mediated spheres, thus alerting us to the tonal qualities of engage-ment as personal individual and collective social experience. Being alert to the spectrum-like character of media engagement – how it can encompass a range of attributes – as well as its protean, evolving character will be a help. Likewise, keeping an eye open for internal tensions and contradictions is always wise. The contingencies of media engagement suggest, wherever possible, the adoption of a flexible and reflexive perspective for analysing engagement patterns and variations in local and global contexts.

NOTE

1   Thank you to Bobby Allen for an insightful suggestion of chordal relations and media engagement.

Part II

CHANGING PUBLIC SETTINGS FOR ENGAGEMENT

3

VECTORS OF MEDIA AND POLITICAL ENGAGEMENT

In this chapter, we reflect on the histories of some compelling political engagement, with an emphasis on the USA and Western Europe, from the 1960s and moving forward to today. We should keep in mind, however, that protest movements have a much longer history. Indeed, in his classic, critical history of the USA, Zinn (2005/1980) shows how contestation of many groups over power has characterised US history from the beginning. Further, to highlight protests is not to deny the presence of engagement in, say, party politics – protests often sought to impact on party politics. Rather, illustratively charting protests puts fluctuations in the degrees and intensities of engagement in clearer relief. In these historical glimpses, we identify some of the major strands to provide a sense of how political engagement via media has varied in form and fervour under differing societal circumstances; it has ranged from intensive mass mobilisations on a global scale to periods of relative quiescence. To understand such vicissitudes of subjective engagement and objective participation, one must look at a range of contextual factors, background contingencies

DOI: 10.4324/9781003179481-5

including major political fluctuations and not least the character, use and potential of the media.

We take a brief look at some of the major protest movements of the 1960s, highlighting some of the complex factors that lay behind these years of intensive engagement. By the early to mid-1970s, the scope of such activism had begun to ebb. Even if there were still many engaged groups, there was a new climate in several countries that signalled palpable degrees of disengagement that stood in clear contrast to the previous decade. We explore this development in the second section of the chapter. The third section charts the re-emergence of widespread political engagement in the 1990s, such as World Social Forum, and at the end of the first decade of the millennium, such as the Arab Spring, Occupy and the environmental movement. Bursting out from the opposite end of the spectrum at about the same time in several countries were versions of right-wing extremism, nationalism and populism. But we begin our overview by noting a rather odd political moment that appeared in the mid-1970s.

AN 'EXCESS' OF ENGAGEMENT

In 1973, a so-called Trilateral Commission was founded, funded by millionaire David Rockefeller, to promote more cooperation between North America, Western Europe and Japan. This Commission was especially interested in young people and their engagement in politics. The Commission published a controversial study in mid-decade (Crozier, Huntington and Watanuki 1975), where the authors discussed what they saw as 'an excess of democracy' – too many people putting too many demands on the system, hereby endangering 'governability'. They were worried that the young were not being properly 'indoctrinated' by the institutions responsible for this task. Unsurprisingly, this document triggered much criticism; it was seen as an expression of the global elite's desire for quiescent citizens, and for a young generation that could be controlled and would not disrupt societal stability.

The Trilateral Commission's study (Crozier et al 1975) is a major benchmark regarding political (and cultural) engagement: during the previous decade, there was intense international engagement from certain segments of society not only about formal political issues and decisions, but also about the character of society and about culture, values, lifestyle and identity. The key phrase 'excess of democracy' was indicative of a sense that some proper limit of engagement had been passed. Though it mainly reflected the anxieties of international elites, this study also had broader relevance, for by the 1970s the scope and intensity of the major protest movements had peaked. As a foundation for future sociological study and for policy reflection, it no doubt retained some pertinence.

While those citizens who are most engaged actively participated in some ways, this does not mean that engagement was absent from broader sections of the population. Films, television series and much music, for example, gave cultural expression that had political connotations and thus brought larger groups of the population into the orbit of contemporary political contestation. Political engagement, as well as group identity and belonging, was also expressed symbolically, via clothing, hairstyles, slang, music genres and adherence to subcultural norms and values in regard to sexuality, drugs and other life style issues. These logics of course continue today, underscoring ever-shifting subjectivities and their links to engagement and participation.

While popular culture could diffusely feed into political engagement during these years of intense activism, most societal communication took place via the mass media. In particular, politics was communicated by mainstream journalism – whose representations largely tended to support the status quo. Here people could see coverage of demonstrations, police behaviour, military actions, debates and so on. Yet mainstream journalism – albeit mostly inadvertently – could also serve to mobilise engagement against official policies: that the dramatic coverage of the Vietnam War on US television contributed to turning opinion against the war around 1968 is a classic illustrative case (see Gitlin 2003/1980, for a discussion of the importance of live television coverage in this regard).

Yet there was more than just mainstream journalism at hand even in this pre-social media era: engagement could be expressed and represented by movement newsletters and pamphlets, student flyers, underground newspapers and magazines and local radio stations. And of course the telephone served a vital one-to one-communication function. However, personal bonding, the sharing of experiences, the building of collective identities that could help carry engagement over to participation required much face-to-face contact, even if the telephone and personal letters were also useful. Engagement had indeed proved to be a complex nexus – and in the early 1960s, political and social circumstances had mobilised engagement and propelled participation – an ascent that came to profoundly trouble the Trilateral Commission.

A Time of Engagement

This section offers a brief overview in broad brushstrokes of Western democratic politics and civil society movements in order to understand varying vectors of political engagement over time. Beyond formal politics, there is the vast terrain of extra-parliamentarian, or alternative politics, comprised of movements, civil society organisations, networks and activist groups engaged in particular themes or with specific issues that can engage citizens. The interplay between parliamentarian and extra-parliamentarian politics helps maintain the vitality of democracy, generating a dynamic that can help avoid stagnation. In the Western democracies, the degree of subjective engagement – and objective participation – have varied over the years. During the mid-1960s, many countries around the world entered into a period of political, social and cultural contestation that was to last through much of the following decade.

The various vectors in this turmoil had their respective historical antecedents, but in some cases, they were also intertwined, for example, some activists from the civil rights movement also engaged against the Vietnam War. Many of these movements generated extensions where we can see engagement still manifested today, for example, Black Lives Matter is a contemporary continuation of the struggle for civil rights. That so many currents came together in the space of just a few years can be explained in part by contextual factors of geopolitics, demographics, socioeconomic development and not least media. After the Second World War, the USA emerged as the dominant global power, seriously challenged only by the Soviet Union in the intensifying Cold War. From this hegemonic position, the USA could spread ideas, education, media and so on around the world – even seeping into the Soviet bloc. Also, after the war, there was an enormous increase in births in several countries, creating a large generational cohort born in the years after 1945. In these countries, relative peace and increased prosperity were definitive attributes in these years; this affluence allowed some families to enter the middle class for the first time. This affluence was also expressed in the increase in higher education that became available. Especially in the USA, more young people were completing high school, and the numbers at colleges and universities swelled. This provided a setting for young people to question the moral compass of a nation where so many citizens were excluded from this new affluence, while its military engaged in interventions and war abroad. It was in this context that television played such a key role in the 1960s. This medium provided a degree of shared perspectives in viewing the world, including both the ideal of higher material standards and the normative vision of democracy (regardless of the inadequacies of fulfilling this vision in the USA itself).

Obviously, not all political engagement across the globe can be painted with the same broad brushstrokes; there always were – and are – national specificities. Thus, in France, in May of 1968, student protests became allied with the discontent many citizens felt, not least workers. This volatile combination nearly brought down the government. In the Soviet bloc, engaged activism against the system had already emerged in the 1950s, with worker uprisings in East Germany in 1953 and the Hungarian Revolution in 1956. In Poland, during March 1968, student protests against restrictions on the freedom of speech and civil liberties engendered a major political crisis. In June, students in Belgrade organised mass demonstrations. In August of the same year, tanks and troops of the Warsaw pact, led by the Soviet Union, moved into Czechoslovakia to crush what had become known as the Prague Spring that strove for progressive reforms of the oppressive system. Militarily overwhelmed, the engaged citizens of Czechoslovakia responded with symbolic expressions of (passive) resistance. In Latin America, citizen protests brought about brutal repression in Mexico, Brazil and Argentina, among other places. Indeed, with the intensification of protests, many governments across the world stepped up their repressive tactics in response.

In the USA and Western Europe, more sustained engagement could be observed in movements that carried on for several years in the 1960s and into the early 1970s. These movements shared beliefs that societal change and social justice could be attained through civic activism, yet it should be kept in mind that within each movement there were various groupings with competing perspectives on how to analyse the problems and which goals and strategies were most suitable. The internal differences could at times become contentious – and even become public knowledge – but the outward appearance of unity mostly held. What follows is a very brief look at some of the major movements for political and social change at this time in the USA and Western Europe.

THE CIVIL RIGHTS MOVEMENT

In the 1960s, a new momentum was built up, fuelled by many years of grassroots organising by civil rights groups and anti-war movements. For example, the massive March on Washington in 1963 put the black rights movement squarely on the American political agenda. The struggle for racial equality and justice goes back to the days of slavery and the efforts of the abolitionists before and during the Civil War to end this barbaric practice. (For recent histories, see Kendi 2017; Dierenfield 2021; Holt 2021). During World War I, Afro-Americans served on the front lines in Europe. Together with the positive treatment some felt they received from civilian populations in Europe; this inspired many returning Black veterans to deeply question the racial injustices of US society, spreading such sentiments further into the black communities. Afro-Americans began building national organisations to lobby, resist and campaign for equal rights as well as ethnic pride; the National Association for the Advancement of Colored People (NAACP) was the foremost of these. During the Depression of the 1930s and into World War II, more black protests and white repression followed; the year 1943 witnessed more than 240 race riots in the USA, while newspapers with black readerships launched a campaign for 'double victory' – over fascism abroad and racist oppression at home.

The movement embodied a number of different political orientations, including the revolutionary Black Panthers, the separatist Nation of Islam, but the dominant one was led by Rev. Martin

Luther King, who argued for a stance of non-violence. Even before he was killed in 1968, major riots had exploded in many of the black inner cities of the USA, fed by frustration and rage; these continued after his assassination. Despite much opposition, the civil rights movement accomplished much, and in judicial terms, its major long-lasting achievement was the passing of the Civil Rights Act in 1964, which ended segregation, and made illegal all discrimination based on ethnicity, religion, gender or national origin. Today, there of course still remains much to be done.

THE ANTI-VIETNAM WAR MOVEMENT

The movement to end US military activity in Vietnam had its origins in what might loosely be called the student movement of the early 1960s. Across US campuses, students had begun organising to oppose societal ills such as poverty, racism and restrictions on freedom of expression on campuses. The notion of participatory democracy, while not always rigorously defined, often served as a guiding light. Thus, by the time the US military involvement began to seriously escalate in 1964 (the first 'advisors' to the South Vietnamese regime had arrived in 1959), an embryonic organisational and ideological infrastructure of a new student left was already in place.

On campuses, protest tactics included marches, rallies, sit-ins and teach-ins, where official reports and interpretations were often challenged (Robbins 2007). Suspicions about the veracity of government versions about the incidents that led to the American build-up grew to embrace scepticism towards even the language used by the military to report on developments. Thus, that US troops 'liberated' a village came to be understood that it could potentially mean the village was destroyed. The cover-ups of the My Lai massacre further undermined trust in official versions of reality. With publication of the Pentagon Papers in 1971, the foundations of such mistrust were confirmed: the administration of President Lyndon Johnson had lied to both Congress and the public about key matters concerning the war. In the course of the anti-war movement (see DeBenedetti 1990; Robbins 2007), such questioning of authority became an entrenched feature within the culture of protest.

Mainstream journalism at first sided with government versions of the war, and often portrayed the dissidents as irrational and irresponsible youths. This gradually began to change in 1968. The success of the Tet Offensive early that year – successful large-scale assaults by North Vietnamese and Viet Cong troops – marked a turning point in US citizens' confidence in American policies. Support for the war began to decline – a combination of those who felt it was basically wrong and those who felt it was not winnable. The major journalistic outlets began to shift perspective. Still, the country was deeply divided, and engagement in favour of continuing the war remained strong and widespread; those who supported the war often saw the protesters as 'unpatriotic'. Opposition to the war went global, with vast mobilisations in many countries. Moreover, in some parts of Western Europe, not least Sweden, strong anti-American sentiments arose. The USA finally withdrew from Vietnam in 1975, having failed in its mission to 'save' South Vietnam and prevent a communist takeover. The history of the war continues to engage, with many disputes among scholars. For many Americans and other citizens around the world, the experiences of opposition instilled an awareness of the importance of keeping critical eyes on foreign policy. The experiences also underscored the importance of collective action and the insight that such action can possibly make a difference.

THE FEMINIST AND QUEER MOVEMENTS

The Civil Rights Act of 1964 was a great legal step forward for women as well as Afro-Americans, since it made discrimination based on gender illegal. In the USA and the UK, the Suffragette movements had their origins in struggles in the 19th century, finally achieving the right for women to vote in 1920 in the USA and in 1928 in the UK. While the right to vote for women is a fundamental pillar for a democratic society, it was obvious that women still were far from being seen and treated as equals. In all spheres of life, from the intimacy of the home to the workplace, to education and public life, to control over their bodies, women were confronted by the power relations of patriarchy, which kept them in subordinate positions (Cobble, Gordon and Henry 2014 offer a short historical overview; expressions of engagement are found in Baxandall and Gordon 2000 and Seidman 2019).

By the 1960s, women were reacting strongly to the traditional roles society assigned them. Even within some protest movements, women felt that they were unfairly relegated to secretarial and other practical/service tasks, while men assumed positions of leadership. The women's movement that took shape in the 1960s was a wave that manifested considerable diversity (see Baxandall and Gordon 2000). In the USA, the dominant grouping, represented by The National Organization of Women (NOW), was largely white and middle class, with liberal politics. Other currents combined feminism with Marxism. In Sweden, the focus was very much on welfare state policies, while in Italy and France, there was a greater emphasis on the body and on relations between the sexes. Many themes were emphasised by different groups, including the right to abortion, domestic violence, rape and equal wages. And some gains were achieved, not least legally; in the USA, these included the 1971 law against discrimination in education and the 1973 ruling that women have the right to abortion.

People within gay, lesbian and trans communities – many having experiences in these other mobilisations – began to move towards civic activism (Faderman 2015; Rimmerman 2015; Stulberg 2016). Historians usually cite the riot that ensued in 1969 at a gay bar in New York City, the Stonewall Inn, as the ignition of the queer rights movement. When police came to arrest people there and close the bar, a spontaneous eruption of protest took place. Gay men and women across the USA and eventually in Europe began to organise, with marches, lobbying, debates, cultural work, arts and social activism. There were two major dimensions of focus: the legal battle for equality and justice, and the sociocultural struggle for broad acceptance of their orientation and lifestyle. In addition, for some people, the movement also provided help in establishing self-acceptance and positive identities. The movement continued to grow during the 1970s and onwards, expanding to become the LGBTQ+ movement: lesbian, gay, bisexual, transgender and intersectional, generally united under the banner of 'pride'. In the early 1990s, the category of queer emerged and became a further category of the movement. This term challenges the fundamental idea that (binary) heterosexuality is 'normal', arguing that sexual orientations and identities are socially and linguistically constructed.

MANY ROADS TO POLITICAL ENGAGEMENT

These developments underscore that there is no one unitary movement or organisation representing these various interests. There is today a vast array of issues and struggles, though connections between them remain: from same-sex marriage and adoptions and definitions of 'family' to gender specifications on identity cards and the challenging of binary sexual orientation as a norm. The theoretical horizons of intersectionality have come to emphasise precisely such connections (Collins 2019). From the horizons of today, much has been achieved in regard to legal rights and social acceptance. In the USA and Western Europe, at least in the major urban areas, there has emerged an extensive degree of acceptance. In other parts of the world, such as parts of Eastern Europe and many countries in Africa and Asia, there remains much legal and sociocultural opposition.

These large and heterogeneous protest movements galvanised engagement on a massive scale during 1960s and 1970s; there were, of course, many other more local protests and mobilisations on other issues as well. By the mid-1970s, however, the initial impact of most of these movements had begun to sputter, and the sense of shock to the reigning order had passed. American involvement in the USA had come to an end, Nixon became president in 1972, heralding a more conservative national political climate, not least on campuses. The civil rights movement had major gains, not least in legal terms; it continued its struggles via the courts, in the media, in the schools and elsewhere, but large-scale demonstrations had subsided. Likewise, the feminist and queer movements continued their struggles on many fronts and in many arenas, but manifestations of larger collective engagement in the streets had passed. Even if the core leadership circles continued their activism, a climate of resignation began to materialise among broad sectors of citizens in the West.

THE LOGICS OF DISENGAGEMENT

With some simplification, we can say that though large-scale protests had waned by the mid-1970s, progressive – and optimistic – academic work on political and cultural engagement held sway for another decade or so. However, gradually, grumblings could be heard from political theorists that democracy was becoming moribund. Citizens' perceived lack of engagement – and thus lack of participation – were seen as undermining the dynamics of democracy: apathy was the symbolic enemy. Not only was participation in political elections declining, but even involvement in the associations of civil society was evaporating. Indeed, by the 1990s, a sort of international academic lament could be heard for democracy – and its disengaged citizens. This set the agenda for a good deal of research in the years that followed; this development was given an emblematic rendering by Putnam (2000) with his widely read book entitled *Bowling Alone*. Yet already, bubbling under the radar, as we discuss below, were the signs of a new generation of engaged activism; the contingencies of engagement were already moving in another direction.

In the age of mass-mediated journalism, most people much of the time did not follow news and public affairs diligently. However, if something happened that was perceived as relevant in some way – that triggered engagement – many would indeed pay attention, if they already were part of a general journalistic 'mediated public connection' (Couldry, Livingstone and Markham 2007). Being connected in this way can be understood as a resource that citizens draw upon when circumstances so require. The authors assert that such a shared public culture is sustained precisely by a sufficient number of citizens being 'civically prepared'. To be viable, such connections must be an integrated part of everyday life, a civic habit, we could say, that needs to be supported by a range of institutions and policies (we discuss the notion of civic cultures in the next chapter).

However, the authors underscore a major problem: for a majority of citizens, there is no clear link between having mediated public connection and any sense of political efficacy. Most respondents in their study could see little opportunity for any participation on their part; that door appears closed to them. Many citizens find it 'difficult to build... "plausible narratives of the self" that link citizenship to the rest of everyday life' (Couldry, Livingstone and Markham 2007: 188). Here we hit a sort of bottom line: if even citizens with mediated public connection cannot find a port of entry into democratic politics, then the structural problems truly run deep. Today, with the rise of digital journalism (about half of citizens in the USA get their news through social media; Walker and Matsa 2021), the public experiences a more pervasive mediated connection – or conversely a disconnection – to politics. Thus, media technology in itself does not guarantee more or deeper engagement; there are other factors at work as well.

HINDRANCES TO ENGAGEMENT

Thus, despite all the official pronouncements and admonishments lauding democratic engagement, from the standpoint of citizens themselves there can be good reasons not to become involved, as a number authors have observed (e.g. Hay 2007). Dis- or non-engagement needs be understood in terms of both social structural features as well as the parameters of everyday life, with their psychological and cultural dimensions. People's feelings of powerlessness, and attitudes of cynicism towards official politics, are among the oft-cited reasons for not engaging politically. For some citizens, there is a strong sense that the undemocratic features of modern society – the inequalities of class, gender, ethnicity and so on – render engagement pointless. Politicians come and go, but in the eyes of citizens, important fundamental changes never arrive. These subjective features – usually deriving from objective circumstances – can engender despair and bitterness over one's life circumstances, a sense of having been abandoned or betrayed by the power elites.

Moreover, basic everyday economic realities can inhibit democratic engagement in direct and material ways. The globalised, post-Fordist economies can wreak much havoc on personal, family, social and civic settings: the harsh demands of work life, extensive economic insecurities (the threat of unemployment, low wages and rising costs of social services), put severe strain on some groups of people more than others, leading to economic disempowerment. The work situation at, for example, McDonalds or Amazon is tough, wages are low, and such companies pursue aggressive policies to prevent union organising. For the unemployed, the situation is all the more grim, and the underclass has traditionally remained disengaged from mainstream politics – gauging (often rightly) that election outcomes will have little impact on their life situation. Redundancies deriving from digital automation, reorganisation, outsourcing, declining commerce and other factors have left many people distressed and financially strained.

Such patterns and their consequences remind us that while citizenship is a formal/legal status with rights and obligations (with the latter being too often ignored by citizens), and clearly underscores universalism and equality, there are some societal prerequisites that must be filled for it to function in reality. The much-cited post-war writing of T.H. Marshall (1950) in Britain provided a major reorientation in contemporary thinking about citizenship in this regard. In the context of welfare societies struggling with class inequalities, he underscored three by now familiar dimensions of citizenship that have defined much of the contemporary discussion: the *civil*, which aims to guarantee the basic legal integrity of society's members; the *political*, which serves to ensure the rights associated with democratic participation; and the *social*, which addresses the general life circumstances of individuals. It is particularly the third category, the lack of material underpinnings of citizenship, that is so difficult to resolve.

Tacit social norms can also serve to undercut engagement, or at least inhibit its expression, even if at times the intensity of engagement will compel people to break such norms. In daily life, people can find that there are few sites or social situations where it is appropriate to discuss politics, few settings where they can easily air contentious topics. Such talk can be seen as 'inappropriate', a disturbing element at family dinners, social gatherings with friends or associates, at workplaces, or cultural events. Politics is often something to be avoided; culturally coded contexts can well inhibit political talk, as Eliasoph (1998) has demonstrated. As political climates become more polarised, more infected, people in their everyday lives often begin to explicitly avoid discussion about contemporary issues. Such discussion – with both strangers as well as with people one knows – can become perceived as risk-filled, thereby constricting democratic dialogue and hollowing out public spheres at the micro level. Indeed, finding and establishing contexts for manifesting engagement is not always easy. And from a very different angle, our characters and personalities give rise to an array of less-than-good reasons for non-engagement, such as laziness, selfishness and indifference. The citizenry is of course not exclusively bearers of noble virtue.

Further, there are always a variety of explicit mechanisms used to deflect engagement and participation in democracy. In Western democracies, measures such as gerrymandering, bureaucratic hurdles and even physical inaccessibility to voting are not uncommon. For example, at the time of this writing, Republican politicians in several states in the USA are passing laws intended to restrict voting among minorities and poor people – groups who traditionally vote for the Democrats. Yet even in the absence of such specific obstructions, many citizens find it difficult to find suitable portals into political life.

The arsenal of anti-democratic measures is extensive under authoritarian regimes – with the threat of violence only being the most obvious. Digital media, at first hailed as an unambiguous tool for democratic engagement, have increasingly become a weapon of repressive regimes. Soon after smart phones became available and were put to use by activists, authorities in some Arab countries, Belarus and elsewhere would round up protesters, take their cell phones and thus have access to their lists of contacts. Also, known activists can receive text messages from the government warning them about the risks that engagement would have – for themselves and even their families. In Turkey and India, governments have temporarily shut down the internet and/or social media in order to block protests. Other anti-democratic measures include building spyware in the cell phones available to citizens. In Russia, all new mobile phones sold must be set to use the national search engine Yandex. The Chinese model of a national firewall that cuts off access to foreign social media and other information sources is the envy of many less advanced authoritarian regimes. And with the development of geographic localisation and facial recognition, authoritarian powers have a highly developed arsenal to discourage undesirable engagement.

NEW WAVES OF MEDIA AND POLITICAL ENGAGEMENT

Ironically enough, while concern was being expressed in academic quarters about the lack of civic engagement in Western society, new mobilisations had already begun to coalesce. For example, the environmental movement had seen its first manifestations in 1970, notably with Earth Day in the USA on 22 April, where an estimated 20 million citizens participated, especially in teach-ins in schools and universities. In the USA, Congress passed major legislation, including the creation of the Environmental Protection Agency. Since then, this date has been annually designated as Earth Day. The movement went global in 1990, and today mobilises ca. 1 billion persons in 190 countries (www.earthday.org/history/). In June of 1972, the first United Nations (UN) Conference on the Environment was held in Stockholm, solidly putting the environment on the international agenda.

This movement also gradually saw the emergence of other green political groups and even parties – some of which have entered into the parliaments of their respective countries, for example, in Sweden and Germany. While engagement remained high in many quarters, it became apparent that environmental politics had entered the political mainstream in several countries – with the result that the measures necessary to truly counter climate change, pollution and other aspects of environmental destruction were not forthcoming. In recent years, renewed extra-parliamentarian mobilisations have focused on major international climate conferences, such as the UN's COP26 in Glasgow in 2021.

Engagement had become rekindled, with an increasing number of journalists, researchers, industry representatives as well as ordinary citizens engaging in these issues. Not least millions of children and young people around the world, following the example of Greta Thunberg in Sweden, have taken to the streets to demonstrate. There had been a long hiatus during the COVID-19 pandemic, but as of this writing, people are again expressing their engagement live, in public places. The role of social media here is not to be underestimated, however: they are essential in order to inform, enthuse, organise, coordinate, express solidarity and maintain network cohesion. Indeed, especially in the new millennium, the new media landscape has profoundly transformed society across the board, and the contingencies for media engagement are no exception. We will pick up this theme in the next chapter. For now, we can just mention that the passion of those engaged in dealing particularly with climate change has, as is well-known, been met with at least equal passion by climate change deniers; their engagement is truly intense, though predicated on a different foundation. We return also to the theme of the rational and affective foundations of engagement in the following chapter.

To briefly pick up our historical narrative thread on political engagement, in the 1990s political activism on the Left began catching up with the academic theorising, as it were: social movements on an array of issue fronts were mobilising, with increasing global coordination (especially via World Social Forum). The confrontations organised by activists in Seattle at the WTO Ministerial Conference in 1999 became emblematic of a new wave of protest politics; the critical encounter with neoliberal globalisation was launched, and 'alter-globalisation' became a rallying cry. In the next decade, engagement rocketed on several fronts. After the global financial crash of 2008, the ensuing policies of austerity and the social devastation that followed in their wake met with much resistance. This was particularly the case in southern Europe with, for example, the Indignados in Spain. The year 2011 witnessed intense political protest in a range of countries: Occupy Wall Street movement, launched in New York City, spread nationally and globally as Occupy, and put economic injustice on public agendas. In the Middle East, the Arab Spring challenged several dictatorships.

At this point in our historical sweep, it becomes important to note that the notion of social movements as organisational frames for large-scale political and cultural engagement had become established. Formal political structures are essential, but there is a vast sprawling and ever-changing field of alternative, that is, extra-parliamentarian, politics, that is essential for the vitality of democracy. Social movements are hardly a new phenomenon, but by the 1980s, researchers were seeing new developments. (The study of social movements is a broad field of inquiry; useful starting points are found in della Porta and Diani 2016, 2020, see also Margetts et al 2018.) These resonated with the socio-cultural changes we discussed above in regard to late modernity, in particular the tendencies towards heightened individualism and especially its demands for meaningful engagement, the declining appeal of overarching traditional ideologies, more loose network relations and reluctance to committing oneself to large organisations.

As part of extra-parliamentarian politics (also called alternative politics), social movements aim to influence political issues and legislation within the established political structures, as well as to extend and deepen democracy by putting new issues on the political agenda, making the state and its various bureaucracies and branches more open, more accountable to citizens. Similar efforts target institutions within the economic sector, at work places, and other major institutions, such as social services, schools and universities.

Yet there is more: social movements also began to erode some of the borders between politics, cultural values and identity processes

(Beck 1998; Bennett 2003). Politics becomes not only an instrumental activity for achieving concrete goals, but also an expressive and performative activity. Engagement becomes more personalised than in the past, based on an individual's values. People thus begin to find new pathways to the political. Such movements are typified by single issues rather than on collective platforms or ideologies. Participation in social movements is more ad hoc, less dependent on traditional organisations and on elites mobilising their standing cadres of supporters; it is operative in decentralised networks (Cammaerts and van Audenhove 2003, Downing 2001). Social movements, particularly in the areas of alter-globalisation, ecology, feminism, human rights, peace and social self-help, often mobilise and absorb citizens' engagement, transnationally, via extensive networking.

The new media landscape of course has played a central role in facilitating these developments, as we discuss in the next chapter. The influential study *The Logic of Connective Action* (Bennett and Segerberg 2013) sums up this trajectory; social movements shift the centre of participation from collective to connective action.

The Occupy movement, in part a response to the 2008 financial crisis but taking a much broader aim, exemplified many of the key traits of a social movement, even if its thrust was much more traditionally weighted towards the political than the cultural (see Byrne 2012; Gitlin 2012). This movement is notable in several respects. While it is often thought of as a phenomenon in the streets, it had a very strong media component, one that was integrally tied to the physical assemblage of activists (Juris 2012). Though the movement was reticent in presenting explicit demands, Sachs (2012) posits that the basic political vision was reminiscent of a classic social democracy from Scandinavia. In using the meme of the people, the 99 percent, versus the corporate greed of the one percent, Occupy stood for ideals such as taxing the rich and the financial sector, including a financial transaction tax, rebuilding the economy as a mixed one with a proper balance of markets and government, shifting public funds into training and education and downsizing the military. In short, this was a reformist, not a revolutionary programme, aimed at enhancing the life circumstances of the vast majority.

From the outset, Occupy presented itself as an all-inclusive, transparent movement, one with an ethos of sharing and empowerment, open to all. It was a large and sprawling 'us' mobilised against the one percent 'them', consisting of the economic and political elites. The theme of accountability is underscored: the cozy relationship between money and politics must be broken and the perpetrators of the financial crash of 2008 must be brought to justice. These were aims that large segments of the populations of Western democracy could more or less support. In fact, mainstream media coverage at times was somewhat sympathetic. Aside from tactical issues such as avoiding to specify any leaders and remaining vague about their goals, the Occupy movement encountered difficulty in creating a solid sense of 'we' from the 99 percent – or whatever large portion that might be realistic. This was especially true in the USA, which is so criss-crossed by differences in class hierarchies, ethnicity, geography and so on; the 'we' was too heterogeneous to compellingly engage all groups without reservations.

THUNDER FROM THE RIGHT

At approximately the same time, on the right, the 'populist revolt' had been brewing for a number of years in Western democracies. By the 2000s, movements and parties were growing and organising in several countries, and right-wing discourses have been gaining hegemonic positions (Mudde and Kaltwasser 2017 offer a useful overview). In the realm of formal politics, this is manifested, for example, by the election of Trump, Brexit and the current governments of Hungary, Poland and Brazil, among others. Within the realm of alternative politics, while some groups are just a bit further to the right of mainstream centre-right parties, others are at the extreme, manifesting xenophobia, racism, misogyny, fascism and neo-Nazi ideology. One can certainly find examples of left-wing populism, but today the dominant version is overwhelming right-wing.

Populist engagement often builds on anger and fear, and erodes key features of liberal democracy (Canovan 1981; Müller 2016; Eatwell and Goodwin 2018; Urbinati 2019). At its core, 'the people' are discursively constructed as a virtuous unity, confronted by evil and/or incompetent elites and undesirable and/or threatening 'others', including, variously, racial and religious minorities, intellectuals, journalists and government. The status and power of large corporations remain often ambiguous. The affective appeal is for 'the people' (of course a category that excludes selected groups) to take back what is being lost; visions of 'the pure nation' are often a part of the discursive ammunition. Calls for enhanced engagement can readily at times advocate bypassing constitutional procedures in the name of 'government by the people'; the attack on the US Capitol in January 2021 is a telling example.

Rational political discussion becomes difficult in the face of anger disconnected from factual reality. Extremist right-wing media practices such as spreading disinformation or harassment can endanger the life of democracy (Benkler, Faris and Roberts 2018; Farkas and Schou 2020; Pomerantsev 2019). The untruths spread by anti-vaxxers is a current example, and that almost the entire a majority of the Republican Party in the USA support Trump's claim that last year's presidential election was 'rigged' and thus 'stolen' is another, very unsettling example. Yet the power of these positions to engage cannot be disputed.

Right-wing populism has to a significant degree managed to mobilise an array of deep grievances – economic, social, cultural – that often are legitimate, reflecting failures of liberal societies to live up to democratic ideals, such as universalism, equality and inclusion. Yet right-wing populism also establishes discourses that set an abstract 'us'– 'the people' – against 'them', variously the government, liberal politicians, mainstream media, intellectuals, experts, immigrants and so on, who are seen as the root of the problems. The power of economic elites is largely ignored, and racist scapegoating and visions of 'the pure nation' are often a part of the discursive ammunition with anti-democratic premises. It must be admitted, however, that this we versus them rhetorical strategy has proven much more successful than that of Occupy – despite the extreme right also being far from a socially homogenous constellation.

The dilemmas facing democracy are many and profound (among the growing literature on this theme, see Crouch 2020; Przeworski 2019). There is a sense of growing dysfunctionalism in the older, established democracies, with political gridlocks and much civic cynicism and frustration; many citizens feel the political class is, if not corrupt, at least indifferent to their voices. In several newer democracies, we see drifts towards illiberalism (Hungary, Poland), and dictatorship (Russia, Turkey). Across the board, neoliberal capitalism continues to shift real power away from citizens and democratic

institutions and puts it in the hands of politically unaccountable corporate actors (Brown 2015). Neoliberalism can readily be entwined
with autocracy (Turkey) and illiberalism (Hungary) in various ways,
with the help of nationalist discourses that celebrate 'the people', the
'national will', and the existing 'genuine democracy', while iden-
tifying dangerous 'others' both within and outside the country. In
the West, democratic institutions and culture are being undermined
(McGuigan 2016; Phelan 2014) and political parties as centres for
engagement and participation are eroding, as many observers have
noted (Mair 2013). Moreover, the devastating social consequences
of neoliberal politics tend to contribute to the growth of right-wing
extremism (Brown 2019). Yet these negative developments do not
go unchallenged, as illustrated by a number of alternative political
movements in recent years.

4

PUBLIC SPHERES AND THEIR CONTINGENCIES

INTRODUCTION

How do we pursue the idea of engagement across political and mediated spheres? In this chapter, we first summarise the normative theory of public spheres, which has become a platform for much critical research on the media. Public spheres today are predicated on mediated civic engagement. Yet how or why citizens actually are to be motivated is not so clear within public sphere theory; thus in the second section, we look at affect and its role in facilitating engagement, highlighting its interplay with rationality. From there, we move into the third section, where we introduce the framework of civic cultures, positing that each of the six dimensions of these resources, though vulnerable, can connect with engagement and operate in mutual reciprocity. In the fourth and final section, we bring the revolutionised media landscape into view, and underscore how digital and societal transformations have dramatically transformed the contingencies for engagement. These have provided not only new affordances but also new dilemmas and even dangers for democratic projects and citizens.

It is worth underscoring here at the outset that here is no one unitary model of democracy; there are many versions in the world today.

DOI: 10.4324/9781003179481-6

The structures and dynamics differ even between older, established democracies such as those in the UK, France, and the USA. Likewise, there is no singular theory of democracy; there exist competing normative visions (Held 2006). Thus, in the real world, democracy must be seen as an ongoing project, shaped by evolving circumstances.

Further, there is also a variety of normative models of citizenship. In Western democracies, the classic, the individualist liberal model of citizenship deriving from the 19th century (see Mill 2002/1859) remains dominant. It sees the state's role in minimalist terms; the state exists to protect the freedom of citizens, allowing them to pursue their own interests and happiness, without causing injury to others. A competing model is that of the 'dutiful citizen', who votes in elections but otherwise is rather quiescent. This version is an ideal among those favouring elite models of democracy. This 'lack' of civic engagement is seen as a sign of democratic health, where democratic politics is best left to elected representatives (a view we encountered in Chapter 2).

Counter-opposed to both of these are republican models (ultimately deriving from the French Revolution); these argue for active notions of citizenship. Such normative ideals not only underscore that the vitality of democracy is predicated on civic engagement and participation, but also assert that such involvement is beneficial for personal growth, in that citizens develop as social beings and sharpen their skills for functioning in collective settings. Politics in these robust Republican horizons is seen as something much broader than just parliamentarian conflicts; indeed, Chantal Mouffe (2005, 2013), a major theorist in this context, argues for the notion of 'the political'. This concept makes the case that there is an ever-present potential for collective antagonisms and conflicts of interest in all social relations and settings. The political, in the sense of contestation over material or symbolic goods (such as values), can arise in any social field. This is a broader notion than that of politics, which most often refers to the more formalised institutional contexts. Citizen engagement is thus always an inherent societal force, a potential capacity that can be activated and mobilised to intervene in present social and political arrangements. In short, for Mouffe political conflict is an ever-present possibility (Mouffe 2005, 2013). And thus, it is crucial that we have a functioning democracy, since it is precisely through demo-cratic procedures – both within and beyond parliaments – that we can peacefully resolve our conflicts. And ultimately, this necessitates engagement from citizens.

PUBLIC SPHERES: IDEALS AND NORMS

The notion of the public sphere has been of immense importance in conceptualising the relationships between media, politics and the dynamics of democracy. Versions have been put forth by a number of writers over the years, including by Hanna Arendt (1958), but the one that has been most prevalent is the one by Jürgen Habermas. Originally published in Germany in 1962, it did not appear in full English trans-lation until much later (Habermas 1989); he has updated this frame-work a few times (Habermas 1996, 2006; see also Friedland, Hove and Rojas 2006), taking into account both critical responses (e.g. Calhoun 1992) and the evolution of society, politics and the media.

The basic elements and logic remain, however: the political public sphere is normatively seen as composed of the institutional commu-nicative spaces, universally accessible, that facilitate the formation of discussion and public opinion, via the unfettered flow of relevant information and ideas. In the modern world, these communicative spaces are largely composed of media. Also crucial is the critical understanding of the mechanisms that impede the full realisation of these ideals, ranging from commodification and ideological hegemony to climates of censorship and outright repression. He points to the class biases of the dominant, bourgeois public sphere, and feminist critics (e.g. Fraser 1992) have added the exclusionary mechanisms based on gender. Thus, the framework of the public sphere quickly became a platform for critical media analysis, and it has inspired countless research initiatives since then.

Habermas and those who make use of this tradition have come to see that the public sphere is far from unitary; empirically, it consists of vast numbers of sprawling communicative spaces of immense var-iety, many of a transitory character. Thus, we and other authors are prone to write about public spheres in the plural. At the same time, these multiple spheres are by no means equal in terms of access or political impact. Some are socially and politically more 'mainstream', and situated closer to the powers of decision-making. Others are more geared towards the interests and needs of specific groups, emphasising, for example, either the need for collective group identity formation or the ambition to offer alternative political orientations, that is, subaltern, counter-public spheres (Asen and Brouwer 2001; Fraser 1992; Downing 2001; Warner 2002).

Indeed, Habermas (1996) describes 'strong' public spheres as those linked to formal decision-making – legislative and judicial assemblies – and all the innumerable 'weak' ones: often informal settings that allow not only for the circulation of ideas and the development of public opinion, but also for the emergence of collective identities. While weak public spheres have no formalised connection to decision making, the health of democracy requires the successful mediation between the two: at least some of the views circulating in the vast arena of weak public spheres must somehow reach decision-makers.

At bottom, democracy is built upon the interaction of citizens amongst themselves, and with power holders. Through communication with each other – individually and collectively, citizens shape their views on society generally and on specific issues. To this end, they are dependent on reliable information, discussion and debate. Despite the problems that by now have become integral to the online environment (which we take up below), today's media landscape offers greater possibility for such interaction in any previous time in human history. Further, given that civic interaction is a social activity, it has its sites and spaces, its discursive practices, its contextual aspects. These can be explored empirically; political engagement and talk always take place in concrete settings. Public spheres do not begin and end when media content reaches audiences and/or is diffused through social networks; this is but one step in the larger communication and cultural chains that include how the media output is received, discussed, made sense of, reinterpreted, circulated among and utilised by publics, that is, citizens – who have increasingly become media producers themselves.

Public spheres thus can be seen as a vast array of interactional constellations; some are relatively more permanent, others more fleeting. While it can be useful to think in terms of a 'standing', always-potentially ready general public, or at least publics with fairly stable ideological orientations, this must be complemented with a more dynamic picture of specific issue-publics that emerge, exist for varying durations, and then eventually dissolve. To the extent that the media catalyse the formation of audiences, we assert that these audiences coalesce into real publics only through the processes of engagement with issues and discursive interaction among themselves. In this transnational era, we see the rudiments of globalised public spheres, facilitated of course by the media developments, yet hampered by the thin institutional structures of democratic decision-making beyond the borders of nation states (Volkmer 2014).

MOTIVATING ENGAGEMENT

The traditional perspectives on public spheres are strongly normative, which provides a solid starting point for critical analysis. However, it does not really help us understand the actual contingencies of public spheres: what makes them 'come alive', as it were, how they emerge via interaction, and how such interaction is shaped by sociocultural dynamics. Phrased another way, we can ask: what are the factors that facilitate political engagement? We can begin by noting that the concepts of public and private encompass an ensemble of traditional notions that readily align themselves into a set of polarities. The idea of 'public' is generally associated with attributes such as reason, rationality, objectivity, argument, work, text, information and knowledge (and, one might add, male, white and discursively dominant actors). The private resonates with the personal, with emotion, intimacy, subjectivity, identity, consumption, aesthetics, style, entertainment, popular culture, pleasure and so on (where the feminine tends to prevail).

Maintaining this bifurcation may have some conceptual use, but asserting empirically is quite difficult and ultimately counter-productive, since it tends to occlude the sociocultural connections between them. As Livingstone (2005) insists, we need to see how private activities, shaped by cultural practice, can indeed have consequences for how the public spheres function. In our everyday lives, we always make sense of our experiences, of ourselves and the world around us using a combination of our head and our heart. There is no reason why engagement in public spheres should – or even could – be any different.

Thus, one of the theoretical dilemmas that public sphere theory faces has precisely been that social and cultural evolution continues to scramble, blur and reconfigure the distinctions between public and private. This porous boundary is abundantly visible in the late modern media milieu, with, for example, its blending of politics and entertainment (e.g. late-night TV talk shows) and the presentation of the private self on public social media. Moreover, people's identities as citizens in public spheres are entwined with other identities that are mobilised in other contexts; the boundaries between them are fluid. For example, even our identities in the intimate domain – family life, gender, choices about sexual preferences, abortion and medical technologies having to do with the body – can quickly take on political relevance and set in motion varieties of civic engagement (Plummer 2003, nicely highlights this domain of 'intimate citizenship').

Another problem has been that Habermas' theorising has generally not addressed subjectivity, identity and affect; it has rather emphasised rational discourse. In short, to understand the origins of political engagement and civic agency, we need to look beyond the public sphere theory, into the terrain of the private – or, expressed alternatively, into the experiential domain of everyday life. It is not a question of collapsing the public into the private (or vice versa), but rather of elucidating the dynamics between them, and understanding the experiences and subjectivities that people derive in this interplay, and their relevance for political engagement. Our first step in this direction to take a closer look at political affect.

AFFECTIVE ENERGIES AND ENGAGEMENT

Our everyday lived realities are criss-crossed with affect, not least online, as Highfield (2016) demonstrates. Our experiences range from the mundane administrative to the intimately personal, to the social, to the commercial, to various forms of pleasure and excitement; games and the thrill of erotic encounters may well take us into the realm of the ecstatic. The links between the personal and the social on the one hand, and the political on the other, are easily facilitated; affect flows quite freely. The political, as we mentioned, can emerge in principle anywhere. With the appearance of such contention, there also emerges a 'we' and 'they', that is, mechanisms of collective identity around the issue(s) at stake. These collective group dynamics – these processes of identification – are driven by the emotional charge of affect.

The significance of affect can be understood if we think of engagement as shaped by something more powerful than just ideas inside the heads of individuals, namely, shared social experience with an emotional valence. Affect animates engagement and helps motivates participation; it brings in the collective side of emotionality, as Papacharissi (2014) describes. She emphasises the importance of Raymond Williams (1977) and his notion of 'structures of feeling': these give expression to prevailing cultural currents and moods of a specific historical moment; they are implicit and inchoate, yet can still impact on people's political horizons. Their political character can of course vary greatly; they can unfortunately even manifest unsavoury sentiments. In analytically opening the door to emotions in understanding political engagement, we of course also allow a set of problems to enter that we cannot ignore. There is an understandable fear among democracy theorists of 'the irrational' – history is replete with dreadful examples. Fear, anger, denial, hate, revenge and so on are emotional vectors that can spur engagement and lead to destructive political behaviour. Yet affect also plays an essential positive role in political involvement.

What we submit here is that to become politically engaged implies not just cognitive attention and perhaps a normative stance, but also a subjective involvement, an investment of the self. There is an emotional impetus here; one *feels* strongly about the issue at hand; *this* is engagement, and it can never be reduced to the purely rational. The intensity and the commitment can vary considerably; when it is strong, we can speak of passion – whose origins and power may well reside to some extent beyond the grasp of our conscious mind. Affect may also hover in the collective background, as a defining disposition that may not be explicitly articulated yet still has impact. Stephen Coleman in his research (2013) and together with a colleague (Coleman and Brogden 2020) has with the use of qualitative methods illuminated how feelings and moods permeate the ostensibly rational context of elections. In contemporary liberal democratic theory, there is a strong emphasis on rationality as a normative ideal for participation and deliberation. Such a communicative mode is of course indispensable at times, especially as formal decision-making draws near. However, to insist on this as the overall model for political engagement becomes constrictive. Indeed, the traditional liberal view that sets rationality against emotion is analytically counter-productive, as many have argued (see Hall 2005). We must grasp their interconnections.

At bottom, political affect always has *reasons*, even if they are not always immediately accessible to us; there is some goal or object that is valued. Political passion is not blind; it involves some sense of the good, something worth striving for, and often also involves some notion as to how to achieve it (even if the goals and methods can always be contested). Reasons, in turn, incorporate emotions; a reason for engaging with something always implies at least some degree of emotionality. Likewise, even undesirable behaviour such as violence and aggression are never exclusively the result of 'pure' affect – there always reasons as well (even if they are normatively unsustainable ones).

Political affect in itself is no guarantee of political efficacy. In fact, it is generally easier to express affect than to follow it through with participation and action. Expressing engagement can of course be important for the long-term instrumental goals by building collective identities, mobilising opinion around issues and so forth (or in anti-democratic ways, generate fear and intimidation). Generally, however, it is easier to just express political engagement than to actually participate and get something done. Marichal (2013) examined 250 politically oriented Facebook groups and found that very few of them encouraged any further action in any way. These posts certainly manifested engagement, but almost none went beyond this expressive mode. Collective affect can provide the emotional energy for engagement. Yet we are still faced with the question of how embryonic or low-level engagement can gain momentum and becomes kinetic, how it can potentially inspire genuine participation. Our analytic entry point to deal with this issue is the framework of civic cultures.

CIVIC CULTURES: FACILITATING ENGAGEMENT

Democracy requires some minimal level of civic input to function, even if the specifics of this minimum cannot be identified with any great precision in any given historical context. We have claimed that engagement is a subjective precondition for participation, but what factors can impact on engagement itself? We can specify one overarching 'pre-requisite': that citizens can actually perceive pathways to the political, that engagement even feels relevant. Yet what is needed to promote such pathways? Civic cultures (Dahlgren 2009) is a way of answering, analytically and empirically, the question of what facilitates or hinders people from engaging as political agents in democracy. This perspective addresses the contingencies of engagement from the standpoint of people's everyday lives; it focuses on taken-for-granted resources that are available – or lacking – for different groups of citizens in historically various and shifting circumstances. While citizens can draw upon civic cultures, they in turn also contribute to them via their political practices. Conceptually, civic cultures is composed of six distinct dimensions. From a analytic perspective, each of them can be seen as both a source and locus of engagement; together, in varying synergistic confluences, they can spur engagement toward participation. On the other hand, their weakness, or absence, can impede engagement and, by extension, democracy itself. Civic cultures should be seen as a flexible analytic tool, to be adjusted according to circumstances. Bakardjieva et al (2021), for example, do so in applying it to the new democracies of Eastern Europe and linking it to the emerging civil societies of these countries. Our rendering here is basic and brief; the six dimensions are as follows:

KNOWLEDGE

Suitable knowledge – accessible and usable – about the social and political world, as well as one's place in it, is essential. By 'knowledge', we are of course signalling something beyond 'information', even if information is the basic 'raw material' that is worked upon to yield new knowledge. Education is a major pillar here, but for most people most of the time, the media are the sources of relevant information – that at best can become integrated as knowledge. This is the premise of the 'mediated public connection' (Couldry, Livingstone and Markham 2007) that we mentioned in the previous chapter. The familiar dilemmas and shortcomings in regard to the media are of course highly pertinent in this regard.

Knowledge in the analytic context of civic cultures does not refer to some abstract storehouse, of a 'political databank' among the citizenry, which survey studies at times try to measure – almost invariably arriving at discouraging results. Rather, knowledge here is understood as the integration of new information with people's existing frames of reference – including not least lived experience – to further extend or modify those frames, including even identity aspects. As such, the notion underscores an ongoing constructionist process, rather than some static cerebral archive. And, importantly, in the context of civil cultures, knowledge's main relevance is for political understanding and participation. All 'knowledge' is of course always already embedded in existing discourses and power relations; it is coloured by ideological currents and can never fully be 'objective'. Yet political agency remains absolutely dependent on knowledge process, whatever their epistemological conditions and limitations.

DEMOCRATIC VALUES

Such values to guide one's engagement and participation are a foundational resource. However, just as there is no one unified understanding about democracy, the values that underlie it may at times be contentious. Ideally, such conflict can be dealt with by democratic means – via discussion and debate. While democracy in theory and practice varies considerably across the globe, it is perceived to be generally on the defensive, even in liberal Western countries. Yet in examining a number of international studies on attitudes to democracy and its values carried out by the Pew Research Center in recent years, Wike and Fetteroff 2021 found some encouraging patterns. Support for democracy and its basic values, such as equality, having a voice in political representation, freedom of expression, judicial fairness and so on is generally strong, even allowing for considerable international variation. Expression of significant support was found even in countries with autocratic governments. There is much critique about the performance of democracy – especially in Western countries – suggesting that most citizens there want more and better democracy, not less. Perceived corruption and incompetence among leaders and poor economic development performance tend to reduce the enthusiasm for democratic values. Among people with conservative and right-wing political sympathies, and among those with less education, however, there was a stronger tendency to dismiss democratic values.

Fundamentally, this research suggests that the major problem is not a lack of democratic values (though this is of course an issue – and a growing one), but rather the discrepancy between them and reality. Similar findings appear in a recent study by Papacharissi 2021, which builds on 100 interviews – or rather, informal conversations – carried out in 30 countries of very diverse political colours. In a vivid and compelling way, we hear people respond to the questions of what is democracy, what is citizenship and how might democracy be improved. While here again there was much variety in the responses, she did not find a 'great global disconnect' on these themes that she had anticipated. Support for democratic values is generally high, but the challenge is how they are to be realised in practice – how, for example, people will gain voice in decision-making. The responses, in their open reflections, also illustrate how people think about these issues in relation to their immediate and broader circumstances – how differing contexts shape subjective experience and potential engagement.

Trust. A minimal level of *trust* is required. There are two kinds. The first is aimed at the basic institutions of democracy – the legislature, the judiciary, political leaders, the overall political culture and so forth. Such 'vertical' trust should of course not be total; democracy requires critical reflection, not blind faith. But if there is a large lack of trust, the system begins to totter. Over the years, trust in major institutions of knowledge, such as science, journalism and the media has increasingly eroded, leading to an overarching dilemma for democracy, as we discuss below. The second kind of trust is between citizens who need to work together. There is an irreducible social dimension to doing politics, and a minimal 'thin' trust, suitable for the 'loose' bonds of civic cooperation, is necessary for those who collectively engage in politics. Without this resource, suspicion and fear easily circulate, paralysing potential engagement.

Practices and Skills. There is an array of practices and skills (that are relevant for the practices) that citizens must have access to in order to feel empowered to engage. People need to have at least a sense of possible efficacy. There are many ways of 'doing' democracy, and these can shift and change with circumstances – new repertoires of practices can emerge in new settings, some citizens focus on – but most fundamentally, the practices and skills have to do with communication.

Not all citizens need to be at home in all practices; there are always 'divisions of labour'. All must however be minimally enabled linguistically; also, to be able to work on a computer, use digital media and so on are central, not least for horizontal civic communication – that is, discussion, opinion formation and so on. Some citizens have developed organisational skills, others are good rhetoricians and function well in debates, while yet others may be very capable in communicating with their representatives.

Communicative Spaces. Settings and sites where political talk can take place are necessary for engagement to be expressed, developed and shared. In essence, we are talking about public spheres, which can be large or small, generalised or very specific. While the internet and social media obviously loom large here, we need to also keep in mind the difficulties of the online world we mentioned above, that is, these factors can impede civic cultures and engagement. Moreover, there are other, in real life (IRL) communicative spaces, such as the workplace, organisational settings and not least the home – where communication might flow and foster engagement. (Even if the home is not a 'public' setting, we would argue that if political discussion takes place there, it becomes at least an ancillary public sphere.)

IDENTITY AS POLITICAL AGENCY

Finally, a self-perception as a subject capable of engagement – and even participation – is crucial. People must be able to take on a civic self, to imagine themselves as actors who can engage, participate and can make meaningful interventions in relevant political issues. This is the identity of empowered citizens; it is a bedrock for a viable and robust democracy. We all juggle a variety of identities, a repertoire of different prismatic renderings of ourselves that are suitable for various contexts – as parents, as employees, as members of an association, as a sports team member and so forth. The civic self becomes activated in the face of the political, when societal contestations appear in one's life.

These six dimensions operate in circuits of dynamic reciprocity – spiralling upwards to more robust civic cultures or downwards, where these resources become eroded. For example, enhanced knowledge can facilitate more trust and thereby foster new or better practices;

mistrust may hollow out previously functioning communicative spaces. Civic cultures are strong in that they can help empower citizens, yet these resources always remain potentially vulnerable to structural factors such as skewed power relations. Thus, civic cultures can be subverted by intentional, strategic measures such as unjust legal restrictions on assembly, censorship, unfair socio-economic and educational policies and oppressive policing. The fate of these cultural resources can therefore often become politically contested in themselves (e.g. government restrictions on media to restrict access to knowledge can be rendered politically contentious). Without such access to the resources of civic cultures, citizens' capacity for engagement with the political becomes weakened.

Media clearly play a central role in regard to civic cultures. While they constitute much of the communicative space, they are obviously also essential for suitable knowledge; they also play a role in disseminating, challenging and innovating values, as well as supporting or undermining trust in various contexts. Most practices and skills relevant to engagement have media implications. And especially now, with social media, there is massive 'identity work' taking place online, often crossing and blurring the lines between the private and the public self, as we noted above (see also Bennett 2003). Moreover, we can readily understand how these dynamics have evolved in the transition from the older landscape dominated by one-way mass communication to the interactive character of today's situation. In the age of only printed newspapers and broadcast radio and television, the power to define public spheres was strongly in the hands of a few. Today's media landscape is of course communicatively more decentralised in some ways, even if ownership is very concentrated among the global tech giants.

Mediated popular culture is also of relevance here: it offers access to symbolic communities, to a world of belonging beyond oneself. This can at times be preparatory for civic participation by offering precisely what Hermes (2005) calls 'cultural citizenship'. It can invite us to engage – with both our hearts and minds – in many questions having to do with how we should live and what kind of society we want. It allows us to process, to work through positions having to do with contested values, norms and identities in a turbulent late modern sociocultural milieu, even at times actualising conflicts where a 'we' and a 'they' can be identified – thus ushering us in towards the political.

ALTERED MEDIA ENVIRONMENTS

The media landscape has always been in transition, but the past few decades have been quite tumultuous, with the advent of the digital revolution. In that regard, debates about what we could and should expect from the internet concerning public spheres and democracy were not long in coming after many people began going online in the mid-1990s. Today, much of the initial celebratory crescendos has dissipated. Sceptics such as Morozov (2011) can find plenty of evidence for not putting much hope in the internet's potential for saving or even enhancing democracy. At the same time, others still point enthusiastically to the circumstances where online political involvement can play a positive role (Castells 2012). Margetts et al (2016) take a modestly positive view, but argue that social media, while facilitating collective action, are also altering the dynamics of democracy, ushering in a new 'chaotic pluralism', whose consequences we cannot quite envision yet (see also Anderson et al 2018). In these new environments, the potential opportunities for media engagement become both ubiquitous and bewildering. The transformed media landscape seems to engender an almost infinite number of new public spheres.

As a counter-point to Parallel with all these developments, it is useful to keep in mind that the fundamental pillar and the most traditional institution of public spheres, mainstream journalism, has been undergoing dramatic changes. It has become financially pressed, professionally on the defensive, while audiences all the more attend to news filtered through social media sites (Alexander et al 2016; Peters and Broersma 2017; Carlson, Robinson and Lewis 2021; Reese 2021); also, the Pew Research Centre has produced extensive reports each year in the State of the News Media Project 2004–2021). The rise of 'citizen journalism' and 'hyper-local news' may serve as a complement and/or partial corrective to mainstream journalism's problems (Harte, Howells and Williams 2018), but this heterogeneous realm of activity further blurs the definitions and criteria of journalism, adding to its uncertain future (Franklin 2016). For all its shortcomings, mainstream journalism has served as an essential institution of democratic public spheres (see Cushion, McDowell-Naylor and Thomas 2021) – and its decline is truly troubling (Pickard 2019). The problems of acquiring secure knowledge in the contemporary media environment become all the more pervasive.

MEDIA CONTINGENCIES

In the online environment, there are a number of varied factors that impact on the character of civic culture and its dimensions. In so doing, they by extension facilitate, shape and even also hinder engagement and agency online (see Dahlgren 2013 Ch. 2 for a fuller discussion). We suggest that there are three fundamental sets of contingencies in this regard; we call them social, political economic, and technical contingencies, which operate in complex relations of reciprocity.

The *social contingencies* have to do with the sociocultural patterns that are embedded in online user practices: the communicative norms, the discursive dynamics, the anticipated intersubjectivity between people on online networks (see Couldry 2014). Mastering these implicit rules, or codes, along with having the necessary digital competencies, gives one access to online interaction, as Baym (2015) discusses; this of course can also facilitate engagement. It should of course be noted that these codes vary greatly – there are many differing patterns and rules that vary between groups and subcultures online (as of course is the case in offline settings). Thus, for example, the communicative behaviour expected within a network focused on stand-up comedy will differ from that of a women's discussion group on domestic violence. Moreover, communicative codes can evolve: political discussion in some quarters today is significantly nastier now compared to the dawn of the internet age. The freedom of speech afforded by the internet has proven to be no guarantee for good communicative ethics.

While there is much edifying discussion online, not to mention humour and satire, playful mischief and pranks, it is nonetheless the case that unsavoury talk and 'netbullying' have become more common over the years (in part facilitated by anonymity, which remains an important and complicated regulatory issue). Domestic and foreign net trolls can cause havoc. Increasingly, hate speech aimed at groups and individuals circulates; harassment and even death threats serve to silence citizens, journalists, public figures and office holders. Women in particular are targeted with sexual abuse. This has made the online environment at times not only an unpleasant but also a baleful and dangerous place (Phillips and Milner 2017). This malevolent development adds intimidation to the discursive obstacles one can encounter, and for many citizens mobilises fear and precaution at the expense of the affect that can nourish engagement. It has also become evident how the internet and social media can serve as carriers of disinformation, propaganda, lies and trolling by foreign governments to influence opinion and elections (Farkas and Schou 2020; Pomerantsev 2019; Fabry 2019). Taking into account such realities may well further dampen citizens' media engagement. Thus today, these online dark places and forces are central to the media's sociocultural contingencies, and knowing how to navigate them is an important skill if engagement is to materialise.

Political economic contingencies have to do with ownership, control, regulation and power. As the political economy of the new media landscape gradually took shape, it became clear that the online environment is not the neutral terrain of communication most people had assumed, but a setting structured by highly unequal power relations between the tech giants and users. And in pursuing their interests, these mega-corporations are not always serving democracy (Zuboff 2019). Google, for example, has become the largest holder of information in world history, structuring not only how we search for information, but also what information is available, and how we organise, store and use it; this power has not always benefited citizens (Cassin 2017). Another example is it has been shown that Facebook – recently rebranded as Meta – has been programming its algorithms to reward more emotional and controversial content by placing it higher up on people's news feeds (Vaidhyanathan 2018). Thus, there is a bias towards the affective, the provocative, rage over reason. This clearly can promote engagement – but hardly the kind that best serves democracy. While we as users can make creative use of the internet, we have little power over its how it is run. Moreover, to try to extract ourselves from it, to actually disconnect, is fraught with ambivalence and major difficulties on the personal level (Syvertsen 2020): to be digitally disconnected is very disempowering. Taking into account such realities may well further dampen citizens' media engagement.

One key area of controversy has been the gathering and selling of private data (Zuboff 2019). Here it is not just private corporations, but even democratic governments who are involved in collecting private data on citizens, contributing to a growing system of surveillance (Lyon 2018). Users are put in a no-win position: if they do not agree to the conditions of data collection, they are effectively cut off from using these media. Further, the deployment of digital media for anti-democratic measures was soon strongly asserted in warnings by some authors and continues today (e.g. Morozov 2011; Bartlett 2018); critical authors from varying perspectives such as Couldry and Mejias (2019), and Fuchs (2021), continue to highlight the unequal online power relations within Western countries. As the tech giants begin to integrate artificial intelligence into their repertoire, their capacities and power continue to grow dramatically (Elliott 2019; Webb 2019). This will of course enable them to offer their users all the more possibilities – yet the negative dimensions of this enhanced power will become increasingly problematic.

The *technical contingencies* of the new media landscape derive from its basic architecture and infrastructure. These are manifested in its general network structure, with its links, as well as in the specific technological affordances of given tools and platforms. On the one hand, the abundance of online materials is a huge realm of freedom, on the other a dilemma. Andrejevic (2013) problematises it as 'infoglut': each of us has his/her own areas of interest that we follow, and thereby wall off most of what is 'out there' as not relevant. We each devise our own individual strategies for navigating the daily digital tsunami, which provides a sense of security and control. Yet even as we may adhere to our own personal or collective filter bubbles, cognitive certainty is dislodged by this informational excess: are we missing something? Should our engagement be placed elsewhere...?

The speed of the internet – the instantaneous results – is also one of its dangers, adding to cognitive dilemmas. Finding relevant information can be difficult in the fast-moving high-velocity informational environment, but still more challenging is developing knowledge. This takes time and effort, both of which become easily marginalised in the digital milieu of the 'the ever new': the present becomes devalued as attention turns to whatever will tantalisingly come next. Reflection and decision-making require time (Carr 2014 pursues these themes in depth); the fast tempo encourages spontaneous emotional response (and often even outbursts). The fact, for instance, that in principle anyone can – and certainly in practice major political figures do – gain large following on Twitter and express political views with 140 or 280 characters per tweet means that the time and space for reflection in public sphere discussion continues to be ever compressed. Moreover, this is most easily driven by emotion rather than rationality – as exemplified by the former President of the United States of America, Donald Trump. Political tweets in themselves readily became news – and can generate much engagement for and against.

The overall 'speed up' of (late) modern digital culture has become a familiar contemporary theme, but its impact is particularly problematic in regard to public discussion and knowledge processes: the premises for engagement begin to shift. In keeping with online speed, Gilroy-Ware (2017) highlights all the *novelty* on offer that provides ceaseless unpredictability and excitement of the ever-new. The present becomes implicitly devalued as our emotional energy becomes set for anticipation of whatever might come next. Pettman (2016) argues that it becomes almost meaningless to talk about distraction when attention becomes so fragmented: we move to a situation characterised by serial micro-involvement. This, as Couldry (2014) proposes, in turn suggests that people are less likely to engage for longer periods with any given political issue, let alone long-range policy horizons.

Abundance and speed increase the competition for attention, and as media environments become denser, the odds of getting and holding attention to any message generally decreases. More broadly, concerns emerge among researchers over cognitive stress, lack of focus as well as eroded linguistic and social capacities that emerge from living and working in the online environment with its accelerating velocity (Jackson 2009; Colvile 2016).

PROBLEMATIC KNOWLEDGE

Finding and extracting relevant information that one can trust can be difficult in a fast-moving digital environment, yet what is still more challenging is to develop 'knowledge'. This takes time and effort, both of which become easily marginalised in the high-velocity milieu of social media. Civic culture and thus engagement can become deflected. Decision-making requires reflection, which in turn demands time (Carr 2014 pursues these themes in depth). Positive affect becomes linked to speed and to keeping up with the new, risking to deflect the demands of rational reflection. Broad concerns emerge over the cognitive stress, lack of focus, as well as eroded linguistic and social capacities that emerge from living and working in the online environment with its accelerating velocity. Not least, attention becomes fragmented. This involves both declining capacities for long-term concentration and selective attention against distraction (Jackson 2009; Colvile 2016). These developments raise questions not least about the sustainment of engagement across time.

Moreover, digital technologies are altering basic assumptions of what we mean by 'knowledge'. Manovich (2013) posits that computerisation is capable of translating just about everything into data, and via the use of algorithmic analysis, it alters what it means to 'know' something. He suggests that we are moving towards what he calls *software epistemology*. With, for example, digital code, data visualisation, machine learning techniques, the ever-increasing speed of processors, big data analytics technologies and social media, we are moving towards new ways of acquiring knowledge, and in the process redefine what knowledge is (Manovich 2013: 338). Engagement is always predicated on some kind of knowledge; how these fundamental transformations are (probably already) impacting on media and political engagement will hopefully become clearer in the future.

ERODING TRUST

The challenges of acquiring knowledge in a media environment characterised by infoglut and speed, as well as by new forms of knowledge and ways of knowing, merge with the quandary of trust, also a dimension of civic cultures. This interface has generated a historically new dilemma for democracy, where not only distrust has profoundly deepened, but also the grounds for establishing and legitimising 'truth' have become destabilised. This throws into disarray the basic

Enlightenment premises on which democracy builds and ushers us into an uncertain future.

Distrust in politics and the media has long been with us, but it can be argued that today it has taken on an unprecedented magnitude. Looking back we see that the groundwork for this distrust within Western democracies had been laid over a period of several decades. Deception by power elites had become more sophisticated and systematic, and citizens of all persuasions had become increasingly aware that politicians, lobbyists, corporations and other actors engage in spin, disinformation and even lies (Tumber and Waisbord 2021). This has contributed to a general rise in civic cynicism (Dahlgren 2013).

As scholars have affirmed doubt is a healthy democratic virtue, one that generates debate and deliberation (Hiley 2006), yet all too often in recent years, incompatible and mutually exclusive views of reality have begun to arise, with competing versions of facts and knowledge. This erodes the grounds for political discussion. For some citizens, the experience of such deep doubt in political contexts can dampen engagement; without the sharp sword of certainty, some may well simply back off. Alternatively, other people/groups may make some leap of faith and, regardless of insufficient empirical evidence or reasoned argument, grasp hold of a particular political position or entire world view, with great affective energy.

In this turmoil, a distrust of those media sources perceived to derive from 'the other' has emerged on all sides, giving rise not only to the famous 'echo chambers' whereby like-minded gather in enclaved self-insulation (Sunstein 2017), but also to a sort of epistemic cacophony, where even the descriptions of basic social realities are often contested. While mainstream media in the West have at times cooperated with power elites to occlude reality, especially in times of war, and activist social media on the left may bend facts and stretch interpretations, the all-out effort to create alternative realities has come largely from the right. Right-wing media in the USA are very vocal in their condemnation of mainstream media; Fox News takes particular aim at liberal CNN, and offers a diet that is closer to propaganda than serious journalism. Far right websites and social media, with various orientations and agendas, often go much further. For the supporters of such politics, engagement becomes premised on new ratios of rationality and affect.

In Western democracies, this disconnect of rationality in the grounding of engagement is becoming increasingly worrisome. Coupled with a weak sense of efficacy, it is easy for many citizens' prevailing assumptions to be psychologically stronger than their critical reasoning. Under these circumstances, collective affect can lead people to find shortcuts to deal with the massive amounts of information that confront them and to look for quick fixes for complex problems. Moreover, the gravitational pull of the group identities involved can reduce societal anxiety and reinforce emotional security. In the long run, however, this becomes debilitating for the individual, it fosters cognitive closure of groups, and it ultimately damages the critical role of public spheres, and democracy itself (see Van Duyn 2022). The end station here is where conspiracy theories become the foundation for engagement.

CONSPIRACY THEORIES AND 'POST-TRUTH'

Conspiracy theories have been with us a very long time, but have become more widespread within certain groups and more expansive in their claims in recent decades (Butter 2020; Butter and Knight 2021; Byford 2011; Uscinski 2020). This is by no means to deny the existence of genuine conspiracies, but conspiracy theories thrive on and reinforce prejudices; indifferent to genuine evidence, they in turn resist proof or disproof, but rather flourish on faith. Circumventing rational analysis, they provide their followers with a sense of power – being in the know, as an insider, plus offering easy explanations for various ills in the world. These ills are portrayed as the machinations of all-powerful secret and evil agents – individuals or collectives. For true believers, engagement in conspiracy theories is intense, and largely renders rational discussion impossible.

This development takes us beyond the media and towards other institutions of knowledge production and expertise: universities, scientific research, schools, and the courts. What we see today from the right wing consists of aggressive attacks on basic Enlightenment premises. This is perhaps most obviously illustrated by climate change denial, where the overwhelming scientific evidence is just seen as another opinion or even a conspiracy. Thus, we arrive at what has been termed 'post-truth', which in fact was the Oxford English Dictionary' word of the year in 2016. This refers to a development where emotional appeals play a stronger role in shaping public opinion than do factual evidence and reasoned analysis. There is some indication that this may at times foster a more dialogic relationship between journalism and its audience (Meier et al 2018), but overall, mainstream journalism is confronted with a difficult challenge.

Truth becomes reconfigured as an inner subjective reality, via an affective leap. The emotionally attractive increasingly becomes the foundation for validity claims about reality – and for engaging with the political world. Emotionality also becomes readily amplified by the algorthmic logics of social media. We see such processes manifested not only in regard to specific events, like claims that the US presidential election of 2020 was rigged, but also by more encompassing conspiracy theories such as those promoted by QAnon. This secretive far-right political movement offer bizarre and extensively fabricated narratives and explanations about how the world works. This is clearly a 'dark side' of affect. Conspiracy theories and post-truth do not completely define political life today, but they comprise strong – and troubling – trends.

Much of the analytic focus on populism accentuates its playing to the emotions of citizens – and the success it can have in mobilising them. This is certainly accurate, but we should keep in mind that all politics (including the most traditional party politics), as we have argued above, require private emotion and collective affect to motivate engagement. Indeed, all democratic politics, we would posit, must to some degree be 'popular' in the sense that they attract support. The popular, however, can tip over into populism, though it is not always a simple matter of where to distinguish between the two. Yet when the political life of democracies reach the point where competing interests, groups, and political parties can no longer agree on the fundamental elements of social reality, and their respective media reinforce incompatible descriptions of the world, and when discussion and debate become increasingly difficult, politics becomes trapped in a gridlock. At this point the alarm bells for public spheres, as well as for democracy more broadly, must ring loudly.

Part III

CASE STUDIES IN PUBLIC KNOWLEDGE AND POLITICAL ENGAGEMENT

5

AUDIENCE ENGAGEMENT

RESEARCHING NEWS IN SOUTHEAST ASIA

INTRODUCTION

In this chapter, we reflect on the empirical research process, including methodological perspectives for qualitative research and audience interview design for a project on news engagement. The media context of news systems, communication infrastructures and freedom and censorship in Southeast Asia are part of the background to the interview design and analysis of the data. The key focus of this chapter is to highlight the methodological choices, lessons learned and relearned and the practicalities of using the five parameters of media engagement for an empirical case. This empirical part sets the scene for Chapter 6 News Relations and further audience analysis of news (dis)engagement within the context of the COVID-19 crisis and the family and social relations of news during a particular period of the global pandemic. We are grateful to our collaborators for this project, Jian Chung Lee and Ha Linh Trang Nguyen for their reflections on conducting the interviews and commentary of our analysis of these rich data sets (see Hill, Lee and Nguyen forthcoming, for further work on news audiences in Southeast Asia).

DOI: 10.4324/9781003179481-8

STARTING THE PROJECT

At first, we discussed how news is an intense mode of engagement that is scrutinised, selected and made sense of on a daily basis. We wanted to place emphasis not on the intensity of news content, but on the intensity of knowledge and feelings surrounding news. As Wahl-Jorgensen (2019) has noted in her research on emotion and journalism, engaging with news mixes the rational and the emotional, including emotion used in the crafting of news stories and as a means for citizens to identify with particular news that matters to them. This is not to say that news engagement eschews rationality and cognitive modes of engagement, as the genre's identity is connected with professional values of objectivity and the communication of impartiality (McNair 2000; Allan 2004; Pantti and Wahl-Jorgensen 2021). As studies have shown, citizens tend to mix affective and cognitive modes of engagement when making informed decisions based on news and factuality (Richardson, Parry and Corner 2013: 175; Hill 2007). From this perspective, we started our research design (see Hermes 2012; Kvale 2007) with an understanding that engaging with news would be intensely processed, felt and reflected upon by audiences. In the parameters of the media engagement model, this placed emphasis on intensities as an entry point to the project design.

However, pilot interviews signalled an overwhelming attention to context, so much so that context became a large land mass containing household context, local context, media context, sociopolitical context and global events, a landmass that took some time to traverse in the interviews and preliminary analysis. The contexts for news expanded our horizon of understanding engagement, from the national context of nightly news broadcasts for cable television watched in the home, to the ambient noise of news notifications pinging on people's mobiles throughout the day, to the political spheres of policy on the health pandemic. Thus, we went back to the drawing board and identified that within the parameters of media engagement model, context looms large and takes a great deal of time and reflection in the research process (Gubrium and Holstein 2014; Seale 2012). Context, even the 'context of context' (Brenner et al 2010; Dawes and Lenormand 2020), formed a backbone to our empirical design, in particular how various vectors of knowledge and feeling for news are shaped by context and familial relations.

As this was also a project that was conducted during the global health pandemic, our study addressed digital journalism in a full-blown crisis. Audiences were impacted by the COVID-19 pandemic in terms of movement restriction orders, challenges in healthcare provision, vaccination (dis)information or precarity of employment, for example. The already heavily digitised nature of news, where people can pick and choose from audiovisual content, became even more accentuated during the pandemic period of the research (Schofield Clark and Marchi 2017; Ferrer-Conill and Tandoc 2018; Swart et al 2017, 2022). This meta context placed even more pressure on onto-logical questions of 'what is news?' by audiences themselves (Meier et al 2018; Peters in Bengtsson and Johansson 2020; Lee 2021). For Edgerly and Vraga (2020), the question of 'how audiences in different countries determine what news is' remains an open one, and given the current attacks on news media and fake news, an urgent question within journalism and audience research (see Meier et al 2018; Meijer and Kormelink 2014; Rouch 2020). In effect, a double crisis of news was occurring in our study as trustworthy information, more often than not distributed and read in digitised form, was put under increasing pressure by the politics of the pandemic. Other studies of news during the pandemic also faced this double crisis within the genre of news itself (Bengtsson and Johansson 2020). This trend in social media as a source for news and gossip about current events, social issues and family matters can be set in the challenging contexts of questions of truth and trust in digital platforms, such as Meta, and varying degrees of media freedom and censorship of news in demo-cratic and authoritarian societies (see BBC News 2020; Center for Independent Journalism 2020; Deutsche Welle 2021). In light of this knowledge the term social media news is used to refer to journalistic news items mixed in with updates from friends and family alongside a range of visuals, memes and influencer content for news feeds; this term is used in an attempt to approach the full spectrum of engage-ment with news via social media.

Avoiding Assumptions

There has been some research in journalism studies that addresses the pressure on audiences when engaging with digital news. For example,

Steensen, Ferrer-Conill and Peters (2020) point to an audience turn over the past few years in journalism (see also Swart et al 2022). Of particular note for this chapter, Steensen et al propose four types of engagement: behavioural, emotional and normative dimensions of audience engagement, within spatio-temporal contexts (2020: 1673). This fourfold typology 'accordingly explicates what a more holistic accounting of audience engagement might attend to, when viewed not only from the behavioural paradigm but also from the individual audience member's point of view, and augments this to also account for machine-to-machine relations' (2020: 1674). There are other relations that go beyond the individual audience member, for instance, 'machine-to-company', 'machine-to-cloud network', 'machine-to-media producer' and 'company-to-society' (2020: 1675), suggesting this typology can add to 'common premises for doing media and communication research into audience engagement' (2020: 1675).

One of the overarching reflections that Steenson et al make (2020) is on challenging assumptions in journalism. We want to add to this point by challenging assumptions about a flow of knowledge that goes *from* media and communications *to* audience studies and not the other way around. For example, the extension of the types of engagement to relations between individual audience members and machines, clouds or companies, underscores the journalism industry in techno-social contexts. From an audience studies perspective, theories and methods are attuned to a 'whole lives' approach to news. Such a standpoint has been developed within audience research over time; for example, David Morley's work (1986, 2017) in cultural geography and infrastructures argues for a non-media centric approach to news and environments. Work on news, lifestyle and gossip (Brunsdon and Morley 1978; Gray 1982; Hermes 1984) foregrounded feminist audience research in domestic spaces. Studies of news and everyday life in the 1990s, by Silverstone (1994), or Gauntlett and Hill (1997), were longitudinal studies conducted in collaboration with, not driven by, news stakeholders (e.g. BBC, Channel 4, and ITV) about the temporal and spatial relations of news in domestic households.

One of the values of audience studies is to challenge assumptions, not going into a study with a fixed object of analysis but observing and learning in an ongoing process of discovery. For example, to presuppose that news engagement is about *individuals* on their personal mobile devices can re-enforce assumptions about the digitisation of news and platform-centric studies. And yet Swart (2021: 13) noted in interviews with Generation Z audiences in the Netherlands that 'engaging with the news had little to do with its content. Instead, liking and sharing or discussing news was done primarily with the goal of fostering sociability and connection with others'. The sociability of news and rumours circulating within social media news is certainly something we found in our study of millennials in Southeast Asia, as we shall see in the next section.

USING THE PARAMETERS MODEL

We started out with the research question: *How can the parameters of media engagement model be applied to Vietnamese and Malaysian news engagement?* We learned early on from piloting that audiences talk around news and politics. The interview guide is thus designed in such a way that each of the five parameters acts as themes, and the sub questions and prompts in the conversation loop back in a circuitous manner rather than run in a linear line (see Appendix). The pilot interviews helped us form a fuller account of context, including meta contexts of political and global news, transregional contexts in Southeast Asia and more national and local contexts of news. We used an open definition of news, with phrases like 'what's going on', 'news about the family', or 'entertainment news', so that our participants could feel that all news that they considered to be news was included in the discussion. Not only does this place audiences as the decision makers in what is news, but it helps in questioning assumptions about news and journalism from a Global North perspective (Edgerly and Vraga 2020).

For Lee and Nguyen (2021), the framing of open questions on the definition of news was not without challenges: 'even as we framed questions around more open definitions of news, participants thought back to domestic and foreign journalistic institutions to discuss how they engage in public affairs'; attention to answers, followed by further questions on the details of news led to conversations about 'technology or entertainment, trade or niche websites, and where they get news about friends and family through private messaging groups or face-to-face conversations'. As we wanted to know about the varied dissemination of news, for example, checking news on the trains, and in shared taxis, via smartphones, to news on the television in the main household, we also asked about devices and where, when and how these were accessed on a routine basis. After a few interviews, we quickly realised that our audience members were not so much choosing to check the news but that news came to them whether they were seeking it out or not, either through notifications, social media messages, or through news and rumours circulating amongst family and friends.

When asking about motivations for engagement, we chose to emphasise identities, such as professional, personal, or social identities being part of their reasons for routinely engaging with news. As people in our study felt they were surrounded by news all the time, motivations for disengagement became significant. We also wanted to know if family rituals for news, established when they were growing up, impacted on their daily motivations for news engagement in the morning, at work, or at home in the evening. This led to some questions and prompts about memories of news and reflections on what they did differently now. In this part of the interview, we discovered a mixing of older and new forms of news, and varying motivations for engaging with different news, such as professional motivations for knowledge from national and international digital news compared with familial motivations for watching national television news, together with their parents and grandparents as a nightly news ritual. Such a mixing of old and new media was also found in research conducted on audiences for entertainment platforms in Southeast Asia (Hill and Lee 2021), suggesting that the social interactions for news are part of a broader trend of mixing old and new technical devices in intergenerational households (Edgerton 2007).

Modalities of news engagement was a broad topic in the interview guide, containing questions about the genre itself and communicative modes of news, for example, family news, or entertainment news, social media news and so forth. As context is so integral to the communicative forms of news, this parameter connects closely to the first in the model. The frequent habit of cross-checking mainstream and non-mainstream sources really made a difference to how audiences (dis)engaged with news. Questions of trust, authenticity and factuality intersected with questions of media freedom, fakery and fact checking. There was so much news to sift through that people in our study turned to family and trusted friends to collectively figure out what to trust or not, or what information to question or act upon. Once again, the context of COVID-19 accentuated the significance of mixed modalities of news engagement and the importance of collective social engagement in our sample.

We can see how modalities intersect with intensities in the parameters model. The time spent being up to date with the news, checking the news, then double checking the news again, is an intense experience, day in and day out. Audience members snatched pockets of news time in the elevator, or on the train, pulling out their smartphones to scan headlines, or opening their laptops for longer news items. For this parameter, we focused not only on the frequency of news engagement, for example, long-form embedded engagement, or ephemeral engagement, but also on the value of news time. To get at this aspect of time and news intensity, we asked people how they would feel if they received no news for a day or two and we found some surprising answers. The weight of news in their everyday lives meant it was a relief to disengage, if only for a short 'news holiday'.

The last parameter of consequences of engagement was a challenge in the interviews. The politically sensitive context for news media in Southeast Asia shaped the conversations about political engagement and participation. Circumspection and indirection were common tactics used by our audience members when discussing what they felt were the consequences of news engagement for a broader political culture. We learned how (dis)engagement and (dis)trust were routine features of news and rumours.

Close listening to the audio files and (re)reading of the transcripts helped us tune into the data and see how the parameters assemble; each of the five parts connect together, at times overlapping, and at other times breaking away to become larger sites of analysis (e.g. context). People made the connections across these parameters for themselves, for example, connecting context, motivations with consequences of news engagement in their hopes for a news that is different from, more trustworthy than, what they have now. In the next section, we focus on the context of news, the first in the parameters of engagement, before turning to a thematic analysis of the negation of news, family and news relations in the material setting of the household, and the relational affordances of news in trusted and tight-knit digital news groups.

SOUTHEAST ASIAN NEWS CONTEXTS

Previous studies have tended to analyse news in terms of macro perspectives on journalism and news practices in Southeast Asia (e.g. Kenyon 2010; Loh and Khoo 2002; Wong 2019; V.T. Le 2018;). Typically, methods from the behavioural paradigm, or uses and gratifications, have been used to analyse news consumption, or credibility, among Malaysian audiences (Omar 2014; Salleh 2012; Zulkafli, Omar and Hashim 2014). As opposed to this top-down perspective on news audiences and countrywide developments in journalism, we use a bottom-up perspective. We set out to explore news engagement by qualitative interviews that tuned into audiences' different knowledge and feelings for news, focusing on the household environment, and how engagement is enmeshed with the relational affordances of news.

In terms of sampling, we used a combination of quota and snowball sampling (Bhattacherjee 2012), focusing on getting an in-depth analysis of a predefined quota of urban millennials. The study participants included 11 Vietnamese and 20 ethnically Chinese Malaysians currently residing in their respective home countries, born between 1981 and 1996 (see Dimock 2019).[1] For the Malaysian study, there were 11 females and 9 males, with occupations ranging from student, researcher and teacher, to dentist, church worker, sales person, journalist and non-governmental organisation (NGO) worker. For the Vietnamese study, there were six females and five males, with occupations ranging from marketing, design, video production, to travel, banking, and the business sector. Most lived in, or near, the two major cities of the Malaysian capital, Kuala Lumpur, and the southern Vietnamese Ho Chi Minh City, urban areas with a high density of smartphone penetration (Statista 2020).

A note on ethnically Chinese Malaysians, these are the largest ethnic minority in the country (Department of Statistics Malaysia 2020).[2] According to Lee and Nguyen (2021): 'political marginalisation and affirmative action, intended to level the economic playing ground between different ethnicities but generally favouring the

Malay majority, have contributed toward Chinese Malaysian identification with being "internal outsiders" within the country' (see E.K.B Tan 2001 for more information on the New Economic Policy). In our sample, audience members and their families read a combination of Chinese-language newspapers, and English or Malay-language newspapers (George 2007), reflecting mixed modes of news that address their multiple identities inside and outside the region.

We recruited participants who routinely engaged with diverse forms of news, combining different journalism traditions, from development journalism, with associated criticisms of government-controlled news media (Kalyango et al 2016; Wong 2004; Gallup 2015), to alternative online news publications, such as *Malaysiakini*, which adopt a form of watchdog journalism, and international news, such as BBC. Our audience members are part of a media generation (Bolin 2017) that grew up with, and are still engaged with, mainstream news, but their preferred mode of news is from digital sources (Ng and Omar 2020: 90; see also Worldometer 2020). As Lee and Nguyen (2021) note:

> This particular generational cohort would have grown up with the affordances of the internet. For instance, Vietnamese increasingly depend on social media platforms to get their news while, at the same time, have had to face stricter state controls upon expression and access online (Pew Research Center 2018). Malaysians within this age range would also have experienced the political tumult that has contributed toward a declining trust in traditional news media and increasing use of alternative, online news media (George 2005; Ng & Omar 2020).

Internet penetration in both countries has rapidly increased over the last decade. There was a significant jump in internet use for the Vietnamese population, from around 30 percent to almost 70 percent from 2010 to 2019; similarly, the percentage of the Malaysian population using the internet during the same timeframe went from 56 percent to over 80 percent (World Bank 2020a; World Bank 2020b). With regard to news, over 80 percent of Vietnamese, aged 19–29 years old, checked the news on social media several times a day, compared to 44 percent for 30–49 year olds (Pew Research Center 2018). Similarly, Malaysian use of smartphones for checking the news is around 80 percent in 2020, in line with internet penetration for the population as a whole (Nain 2020).

The historical and political background to news provision in Malaysia is complex; what follows is a brief account (with references for further reading). Broadcasting and publications acts established in the 1980s require publishers and broadcasters to acquire/renew their licenses with the Malaysian Home Minister (Loh and Khoo 2002: 126). The Printing Presses and Publications Act of 1984 and the Broadcasting Act of 1988 are directly tied to the operations of print and broadcast media, but there is also the Sedition Act of 1948 that has contributed toward a restrictive media environment (Loh and Khoo 2002). Further political control of the media is exerted through ownership, for example, the former ruling government Barisan Nasional ('National Front' in English) has invested heavily in print media ownership, directly influencing editorial and news content (Kenyon 2010). Lee and Nguyen note (2021):

> Malaysia has one of the lowest percentages of trust in news among the 40 countries surveyed in the 2020 Reuters Digital News Report, as only 25 percent of those sampled said "they trust most news most of the time" (Nain 2020). This distrust is cited as one of the contributing factors to younger Malaysians disengaging with traditional news sources, specifically because they see them as government controlled and advancing "official government viewpoints" (Ng and Omar 2020: 92).

For the millennial Malaysians in our study, they turn to non-mainstream news on a daily basis (see also Lee and Fathin 2018; Lee 2019; Yunus 2020). The infrastructures for digital and alternative news are significant in Malaysia as it supports a thriving non-mainstream news scene. Early investment in the Multimedia Super Corridor (MSC) initiative enabled Malaysia to open up digital dissemination of news (Ng and Komiya 2002), significantly applying a less draconian, legal framework drawn up by the then ruling Barisan Nasional government (10-point Bill of Guarantees; George 2005: 910). Chinnasamy (2018) highlights how this communications infrastructure enabled digital and citizen news media to circumvent a range of licensing agreements. George (2005: 910) contends that non-mainstream Malaysian news tapped into a network of mutually beneficial 'political parties, civil society groups, non-government organizations' and supporters. At the same time as the Reformasi (Reformation) protest movement, non-mainstream news websites such as *Malaysiakini* and *Harakah Daily* were also founded (Chinnasamy 2018).

Registered news outlets in Vietnam are controlled by the Socialist Party; the Central Propaganda and Training Commission and the Ministry of Information and Communication (under the Vietnamese Press Code 2016) controls news that promulgates the political agenda of the governing party (Mach and Nash 2019). Control is manifested through a series of measures that assert the power of the party, from meetings with journalists and officials, weekly reviews of news content by the Ministry of Information and Communications, to complaints, fines and penalties, for example, replacing editors or shutting down websites.[3] These strictures on media freedom serve to enforce state power and promote the political agenda of the governing party (Mach and Nash 2019; Hayton 2010; see also Reuters 2021b; South China Morning Post 2020). The type of print and broadcast news tends to cover 'commercially rewarding but politically benign content' (Nguyen-Thu 2018: 989). In addition, reduced revenue from the state has led to commercial partnerships and editorial agendas that favour headline-grabbing stories (Heng 2002).

This brief overview of national news media sets the scene for the rise in mobile social media publics. Citizen journalism and bloggers have been able to cover news that has drawn younger Vietnamese audiences to their sites, for example, 80 percent of Vietnamese, aged 19–29 years old, checked the news on social media several times a day, compared to 44 percent for 30–49 year olds (Pew Research Center 2018; see also Linh 2021; Nguyen 2019; Nguyen et al 2018; Pham 2020). This picture of mobile social media news as a space for citizen participation is offset by the regime's response to bloggers (see Le 2014; Le 2018; Bui 2016; Nguyen 2014). According to Lee and Nguyen (2021):

> The Vietnamese government has also taken punitive measures, including imprisonment, against both bloggers and journalists (Duong 2017). In addition to this, the Cyber Security Law of 2019 allows the government to demand that Google or Facebook provide them with

personal information on Vietnamese users; censor posts deemed wrong or contributing toward "social disorder"; and limit access to offending individuals or organizations (Mach and Nash 2019: 4).

And a sense of social media news as a resource for social resilience is complicated by the uptick in online Vietnamese nationalism (Nguyen 2021), as evidenced by the regime's use of platforms such as TikTok for news, or the co-optation of social media news by political elites (Duong 2017). Such a news climate creates an ambivalent situation for (dis)engagement with news and civil society by young Vietnamese audiences (see also Wells-Dang 2014; Park 2019). For example, there are general statistics for the population as a whole that state that nearly 80 percent of Vietnamese claimed that the news media was accurate and covered politics fairly, with 85 percent claiming that they were satisfied with the coverage of important events in the country (Pew Research Center 2018). And yet, what lies behind these statistics is unclear as there is little qualitative research on Vietnamese news audiences.

RESEARCH REFLECTIONS

As discussed earlier, methods and theories of how to study news audiences can be found in early research on audiences and domestication (e.g. Morley 1986) and contemporary research in journalism (e.g. Rouch 2020). The double crisis of news during the COVID-19 global pandemic only serves to emphasise that research on engagement is essential if we want to understand how citizens access, process and act on information, be it the health crisis and significance of trustworthy information for the public, or the crisis within journalism and the ongoing problem of fake news and disinformation. During the COVID-19 crisis, the pressure on the practice and meaning of news engagement increased exponentially.

In their fieldnotes and reflections on conducting the interviews, Lee and Nguyen (2021) offer insights into the practice of news engagement. As an ethnically Chinese Malaysian, raised in one of the surrounding neighbourhoods of Kuala Lumpur, Lee was familiar with participants' experiences with news. They recalled the 'rolled-up copy of *The Star* from the delivery person in the morning' as part of their childhood, or watching nightly news reports with their family. They too experienced an emotional rollercoaster of social protest, for example, the yellow march through the capital Kuala Lumpur on political corruption (Reuters 2016), to political change and disappointment, for example, the first change of government in more than 60 years (only to crumble two years later; Head 2020). Conducting the interviews during the global pandemic underscored how news is contested, amplified and needed by Malaysian citizens.

> In WhatsApp groups, they question why this family member or that friend continues to share misinformation regarding COVID-19 infections, vaccinations and even home remedies. Some wrestle over whether they should say something in response or to throw their hands up as the stream of misinformation carries away the conversation.
>
> (Lee and Nguyen 2021)

For Lee and Nguyen, the political context pushed participants to 'draw a line between news on the governance of the country and the bickering between political interests'. For example,

> Malaysian news on former Prime Minister Muhyiddin Yassin declaring a state of emergency and suspending parliament (Sukumaran, 2021) holds their attention. News on the in-fighting and the pulling of support within his ruling coalition, ending in his resignation, (Yi & Yusof, 2021) simply becomes background noise.

The political context in Vietnam pushed participants to look for foreign news as a counterweight to news propaganda.

> Being born in a country where news is strictly censored by one party government meant that participants had limited access to news that contained different perspectives on political or social issues, and were not encouraged to talk about politics or share opinions.
>
> (Lee and Nguyen 2021)

The impact of news during the pandemic placed emphasis on institutional contexts for news engagement and disengagement. What is more, political dysfunction and the challenges of news engagement in authoritarian societies brought into sharp relief the resilience of citizens as they search, sift through and figure out news they can trust in one way or another.

A final point to make that arises from the research reflections by Lee and Nguyen is that participants' (dis)engagement with news resonated beyond the content of news and information to political and social spaces. If we understand engagement as the energising internal force of audiences to access, read and discuss news, resonance is the quality of news in its meaning and value for audiences at this moment in the COVID-19 crisis. The consequences of their news engagement, the observable impact of news, is another aspect of research related to political participation, social protest and citizen action. As we shall see in the other case study of political protest and social movement in Belarus, the subjective conditions of engagement can, in other concrete examples, be researched and observed in terms of impact on policy, or media censorship, and citizen participation in courtyards and collective solidarity, for example (see Chapter 7).

CONCLUSION

In sum, from the context of news engagement within the parameters model, we find a *default distrust* in mainstream news and routine engagement with *mixed modes of news*, for example, non-mainstream news, digital news platforms and international news, for the millennial audiences in this study. Differences in the degrees of distrust and political talk in mediated and public spaces can be found across the transregional sample. In the next chapter, we explore a hesitancy to talk about news, in particular political news, something that is felt more keenly in the Vietnamese sample due to the greater control of news in this region. This way of negating news and avoiding talk of politics serves to, at times, make news and politics more present by its absence – which leads us to a trusted space to talk about news and politics, that of the home, and family and friends' digital news groups. The family structure, shaped by norms and values for intergenerational and patriarchal family environments in Southeast Asia, illuminates the relational affordances of news. All of our findings are heightened during COVID-19 cultures at the time of the interviews and the meta context of the global health pandemic, which places added pressure on the identity of the genre and audience engagement with it.

NOTES

1   These age ranges are based on the Pew Research Center's definition of millennials (Dimock 2019).
2   In 2020, they make up 22.6 percent of the Malaysian population, followed by Indian Malaysians at 6.8 percent and others at 1 percent (Department of Statistics Malaysia 2020).
3   My thanks to Andreas Mattsson for the in-depth knowledge of news in Vietnam.

6

NEWS RELATIONS

Chapter 5 introduced the research design and methodological considerations for an empirical study of news and audience engagement. In Chapter 6 we now connect the empirical reflections on research processes to the analytical findings of the case. As mentioned in previous chapters, the significance of context and contingencies becomes crucial to how the parameters work as an empirical model. Context connects the parameters together, indeed sets an overall tone to the parameters as a whole. The specifics of this case study of news engagement in Southeast Asia (see Figure 6.1) may on first reading seem somewhat outside the realm of media engagement we are familiar with, such as in democratic systems and journalism practices in the Global North. We ask readers to consider this case with regard to their own spectrum of engagement and media experiences in other situations and regions, and in different COVID-19 cultures and post-pandemic societies. The case is an example of disengagement with news and information, with unusual degrees of power over citizens and publics in different media and public orders for Malaysia and Vietnam. The case is also a good example of broader patterns for news engagement and mobile social media publics: it illustrates

DOI: 10.4324/9781003179481-9

Figure 6.1 'Street news' © 2017 Zaki Habibi/Photograph by Zaki Habibi

how the local and the global connect together, underscoring examples of homogeneous media engagement, e.g. patterns that are similar across transregional news audiences, and heterogeneous engagement, e.g. patterns that differ in degree or tone. Here, then, the local and global perspectives on news relations are highly attuned to our way of understanding the significance of media contexts (Peck 2010, 2020) that colour the parameters of media engagement.

FORMS OF KNOWLEDGE AND PRACTICES OF KNOWING

An odd moment in the thick of fieldwork. An hour long interview about news becomes an hour and half long talk around and about the topic of news and rumours. For example, a former news intern: 'I honestly don't keep up with Malaysian politics. I find it depressing; a political journalist on Malaysian social media news: 'it's a waste of time to engage' or; a Vietnamese PR account executive on smart-phone news: 'from the elevator to my desk, or when I walk to the pantry, I'm stuck to my phone. I read while I am walking'. In those moments another voice resonated strongly: not a news voice, but a creative voice from a novel.

The voice in *Milkman* by Anna Burns (2018) is striking; a young char-acter living in a hair trigger society, scarred by partisan politics and war; a character driven narration that goes around and around rather than taking a straight course; and a voice from a community barely getting by in an authoritarian society (1970s Northern Ireland). *Milkman* 'records a voice of someone who has struggled to find that voice' (Hutton 2019: 367). The main character of 'middle sister' has no name; and in fear of wrongly labelling anyone, anything and anyplace that can be interpreted wrongly by people, they avoid naming altogether. The 'opaque quality' of the narrative is a distinctive feature: the processes of negation, of not naming and of circumlocution are all part of living with the continual threat of harassment, coercion and violence in a dysfunctional family and societal environment (Hutton 2019: 360). The smallest of details can be used against people by the local community, informers or state actors. For example, middle sister's habit of 'reading-while-walking' makes others suspicious of them, so much so that this habit makes middle sister an object of attention, a subject of local gossip and a target for perpetrators of violence.

The enmeshment of voices from the audio interviews with the fictional narrative voice of this novel tells us something about what we can learn from people who struggle to find a voice. The focus in this chapter is on a specially designed audience research project that explores the five parameters of media engagement, from context, motivations and modes, to intensities and consequences of engagement (see Chapter 5 for full details). Two researchers (Lee and Nguyen) helped us craft an audience project that addressed news in Southeast Asia, with a quota sample of thirty young millennials in urban cities. We started out interested in the current environment for news within the context of media and society in Malaysia and Vietnam. But, what we found was something else. The people in our study often started out claiming they were not going to be very interesting subjects for an interview, nor did they really engage with the news – indeed, why interview them at all? Audience members talked around the subject of news and rumours. They would negate their news engagement. And at the same time they would reflect on how news was everywhere, coming to them through their smartphones, transmitted on television, and sometimes debated, other times resolutely ignored, in the family WhatsApp chat.

Corner (2011: 69) argues that media engagement can help us understand forms of knowledge and practices of knowing. With regard to news, diverse encounters with knowledge from journalists, key opinion persons, experts and citizens, for national and international news and social media, connect with diverse practices of knowing. We therefore take Corner's point on 'different vectors of knowledge and feeling' (Corner 2011) as a framework for our exploration of news engagement. Our case study of Malaysian and Vietnamese news audiences means that the various vectors of knowledge and feeling regarding news (dis)engagement are set within a climate of (dis)trust with news provision.

In Willems (2020: 3) research on news and digital media in Zambia she argues for the relational affordances of mobile social media, meaning the relations between an object and actor in situated contexts. We analyse the relational affordances of news for smartphones, laptops, or on broadcast and cable television, where we find not one object or actor, but old and new media devices and multiple actors involved in news relations. We explore news relations in intergenerational households, where there is shared access and distribution of news, e.g. through family accounts for Wi-Fi and cable television, and where news can be a topic of conversation in trusted news groups. Within these familial structures we find patterns of engagement for exchanging sources, fact checking and sharing news, which relates to the theme of news verification. And within these same family settings and digital news groups we also find people starting and spreading rumours, which relates to the theme of rumour refutation. Similar to Willems, we connect the specificities of our research in the Global South in broader understandings of news relations, specifically the relational affordances of news in environments where there are varying degrees of distrust in news and where despair colours a life lived in authoritarian societies.

THE NEGATION OF NEWS

In this section we analyse how the parameters of motivations, intensities and consequences for engagement work together. There is a form of news negation as audiences process their negative feelings about news in the societies of Malaysia and Vietnam. Negating news, from poor quality in journalism, lack of verifiable sources and government control of content in these two countries, is a means of voicing concerns regarding various forms of news and practices of knowing (Corner 2011). For example, a graphic designer (male, 30 years old) offered this sharp critique of mainstream journalism in Vietnam: 'those producing content are not well trained or professional... their content can even kill people'. A Chinese Malaysian analyst working for an NGO (33-years-old male), summed up his experience of reading mainstream news: 'you put two and two together and... sometimes, you know, the opposite is true'. Such comments by these two audience members are situated in the histories of Vietnamese media systems and journalism education during colonial and postcolonial periods (Nguyen 2006), and the complexities of Chinese Malaysian communities and news provision (Loh & Khoo 2002).

By referring to audience negation of news, we mean the definition of negation as something (e.g. news) that signals the absence of something in real life (e.g. trustworthy, impartial or uncensored news). The process of negation also holds the possibility of reversibility, so, being negative about news can also be inverted to a positive about the potential of news to inform citizens. This helps to explain how audience negation of news doesn't necessarily mean an absence of news altogether. Audiences worry about the impact of disengaging with news (what if something happens?) and the civic consequences of news disengagement in the longer term (what about the potential for political change?). Processes of news negation, then, conversely lead to intense and wide ranging news engagement by most of the audiences in our study.

A typical opening for an interview – 'I'm not too interested in news', or 'I take my news with a pinch of salt'. In a pilot interview with a Chinese Malaysian 29-year-old university student, studying a Master's in environmental and food security, they stated early in the interview their negation of political news: 'I'm not too interested in politics, especially in those parties and things like that... sometimes it sounds stupid, so we just take it as a story'. Thus, the interview starts with negation and the political context of news engagement. They go on to explain: 'I don't side, I just see for myself and I won't inform others'. Such a statement fits with a general distrust within this generation: in a survey of 40 countries for the Reuters Digital News Report (2020), only 25 percent of those sampled in Malaysia said 'they trust most news most of the time' (Nain 2020). Young citizens routinely disengage with mainstream news that is perceived as government controlled and advancing 'official government viewpoints' (Ng & Omar 2020: 92). This default distrust in news is rooted in the political context of Malaysia and the government's control over mainstream media content and access (George 2005).[1]

If we consider Nina Eliasoph's (1998) argument regarding American citizens and activists avoiding politics in their everyday lives, this is something that generates apathy in the context of the Global North. However, in Southeast Asia, we find something else is going on – not political apathy, but, as we have noted already, audience negation of news. Having started with the negative declaration 'I'm not too interested in…' this Chinese Malaysian (29-year-old female university student) then noted:

> When I say avoid, I don't mean I totally don't read the news. It's not to say that when I see the news regarding politics I just skip to the next page. I still read the headlines and some of the information inside but I won't propagate it to others. That is what I mean by not actively participating in political issues.

In fact, she engages with various forms of news: 'not just one source but two or three sources, like *The Star*, *New Straits Times*, *CNA* (Channel News Asia) so… if they report the same thing, then I would conclude it as trustworthy. Truthful'. Intense patterns of engagement for national and transregional news act as counterweight to a general disposition of distrust in politics: 'I would verify these issues with the resources that I think are trustworthy, which are the four or more that I mentioned'. This participant went on to explain:

> I'm kept updated with the current affairs. If not, I think I would be, like, there's a Malay word, it's the frog in the well. The Malay term 'katak

dalam tempurung',[2] yeah, the frog in the well. That means you don't know any other thing other than your own surrounding. You don't know what's happening in our neighbours... in the neighbouring countries or, perhaps, in Europe. Who knows?

The everyday saying of the frog in the well, a Vietnamese phrase (Ếch ngồi đáy giếng), is mirrored by the Malaysian saying 'the frog under the shell' (Katak di bawah tempurung). It's a cautionary tale, used to signify the consequence of being oblivious to what is going on around you. The frog in the well, under the shell, metaphor is an example of the kind of detail that connects with Charles Taylor's (2004) work on the 'modern social imaginary', in which metaphors, or folktales, form shared stories by people in their collective shaping of sociocultural norms and values. The social imaginary helps in our analysis of distrust and news (dis)engagement. There was one Chinese Malaysian person who disengaged from all news and found themselves caught unawares in a COVID-19 lockdown situation where they did not know about the latest movement restriction orders in their local community. They returned to this personal experience as a salutary lesson of what happens when you are 'the frog in the well'. The phrase signifies how audience negation of news comes with a salutary reminder of the consequences of disengagement for citizens.

Towards the end of the interviews, we asked people what would happen if they were without news for a day. The types of responses highlighted how being without news was considered a holiday, a physical and psychological relief from the pressures of intense news engagement on a daily basis. It was also a sinister indicator of government censorship and control. For example, Liu, a 33-year-old male journalist, living in Kuala Lumpur, regularly engages with a whole host of national and international news from *Malaysiakini, Astro Awani, The Star, New Straits Times, The Malaysian Insight, Malay Mail, Sinar Harian, Berita Harian*, as well as *Science, Nature, The Guardian* and the *BBC*, all as part of his work covering politics for an alternative news outlet popular amongst our audience members. He felt a day with no news was 'a good day... it probably means that I had a relaxing day', and a week with no news was even better: 'It's probably a good sign because I haven't had that in a while'.

Similarly, this PR consultant who intensely engaged with news online all day felt relieved to be without news:

> I'm actually O.K. without getting any news... Because there are days when I just want to not know anything about the world and to just be in my own world and zone out from everybody... there's just too much news. News is endless.
>
> (Female 28-year-old PR consultant)

Soon, a 34-year-old female director of an agricultural supplies company, reads *Sin Chew Daily* in the morning, news on their mobile anytime she is free and listens to podcasts when commuting to work. She experienced being the frog under the shell and lived to tell the tale: 'I went to the jungle for a month... I didn't have any phone, internet, and I couldn't call out as well, but I survived'. For another audience member, being without news would 'feel like a holiday, man'. She described being 'emotionally dragged down by the news' and, once in a while, decided to be the frog under the shell: 'stop looking at the social media and stop looking at news'.

The pressure of news engagement, from various online sources, was palpable. As one person succinctly put it: they do not check the news but instead 'news comes to me'. Audience members reflected on how they would snatch time to check the news throughout the day, during the morning commute to work, even in the toilet. A 27-year-old female Vietnamese professional, working in a global public relations consultancy firm, reads the news whilst walking from place to place: 'when I am waiting for the elevator, or early in the morning when I arrive at the office and there is nobody there,... I'm stuck to my phone. I read while I am walking'. Echoes of the character of middle sister in Anna Burns novel *Milkman*, who reads whilst walking; this audience member carries the news on her person at all times.

Jia, a 31-year-old female assistant brand manager obsessively checks Twitter, Outlook, Google and Facebook: 'always on my mobile. I'm always on my desktop'. As part of her job, she would travel to remote rural areas in Malaysia with limited access to Wi-Fi, and during this 'sudden digital detox, my head started shaking. I realized that, "no, this is not a good thing"'. To be without news? 'If it is my own choice, then I'm O.K... if it's just a day... if it's something to do with something that is much more sinister, then that is a different story'. To be without news can have dire consequences: 'I don't know what is happening around me. I am scared of losing control' (28-year-old Vietnamese male video producer). Note the neutral phrases ('something to do with something') standing in for censorship, or the darker overtones of being disconnected from the news ('I don't know what is happening around me').

A negation of news involves conflicting vectors of knowledge and feeling (Corner 2011). The meaning of vector as carrier is important here. News, and its normative values of truth and trust, carries meanings audiences associate with reliable sources of information; and yet news, in reality, carries feelings of distrust. For example, this 30-year-old male graphic designer from Vietnam distrusts mainstream news and at the same time intensely engages with news, cross checking sources from: 'official news channels and alternative channels... I will read Vietnamese news channels and international channels... I want to know high quality information'. The vectors of knowledge for this person are multifold as he intensely engages with several sources. But what can he do with this knowledge? He finds himself weighing news on a daily basis – is this enough quality information? How much is the government controlling news and opinions? The vectors of knowledge and feeling about news become heavy with meaning: 'I read political news for the sake of knowing... I should not know too much. If I know too much, I lose hope, so I try to limit political news'. Thus, the consequences of his intense news engagement are opaque: 'I know about it, people know about it, but don't talk about it'.

NEWS ENGAGEMENT AND FAMILY RELATIONS

Hup is a female writer, living with her parents in Kuala Lumpur, who regularly reads *Malaysiakini*, *The Guardian* and *The New York Times*. The interview starts with a negation of news, a discursive frame within which to position herself against news and politics: 'I would make a pretty disappointing participant because I hardly keep up with the news but... just, honestly, the little that I do, I find out via Instagram'. A light engagement with entertainment news sets up a dark contrast to Malaysian politics: 'I find it depressing, the outcome is always not really with the people in mind and... it's just so much corruption'. Later on Hup contradicts her earlier negation of news. At home with her father, she cross checks news sources: 'reading news articles is a hobby. He enjoys it... he's always telling us "if you hear something on CNN, switch to al-Jazeera and CCTV as well to see what they're saying about it and whether or not it's accurate" '.As the interview progresses, she says more about a distrust in mainstream news. 'I interned for *The Sun* because I was majoring in journalism and it was during that internship when I realized I don't think I want to be a journalist'. After this internship she went on to work for an advertising company, with *The Star* as a client:

> I witnessed firsthand, during the election, how they attempted to twist certain pieces of news... some of my colleagues got pulled in against their will to come up with a series of propaganda ads. It was blatantly untrue. A lot of people who were forced into working on those ads were uncomfortable... One of them, to this day, has not told their parents because I think they felt it was shameful that they had to partake in something like that and, after those ads ran, there was a lot of anger because people were, like, 'this is a newspaper, you're supposed to be impartial'.

Hup also went to Bersih protests with her parents, a civil society movement calling for electoral reform (Bersih means 'clean' in Malay). The news reports of the movement were a source of concern: 'I was at Bersih... the way it was reported in *The Star* was very odd. It was just... blatantly untrue... I don't think any of us felt comfortable continuing to subscribe'. Her negative experience was shared with 'my other relatives, like my aunties and stuff' and this became a source of outrage: 'they got angry... I knew there was distrust – they talked about it – but yet they never cut the subscription before... They kept it up until they felt, "O.K. this is the last straw. It's clearly a lie" '. A series of factors, from growing up in a family that values news engagement, to negative experiences within the communications profession and participating in a social movement, all serve as catalysts for questioning news bias and misrepresentation. When one family member stops their subscription to *The Star*, others follow suit: 'this is the last straw'.

The significance of the family for understanding news and political engagement is important. Audiences would recall growing up in households where their father would encourage reading the news and checking sources, reflecting the familiar authority figure of the father in Chinese Malaysian and Vietnamese households, a figure that is part of change and continuity in these domestic settings (Cheah et al 2018; Rukmalie and Phuong 2013; King et al 2008). Not only did Hup learn from her father about modes of news engagement, e.g. comparing sources, she also learned that the family home was a trusted place to talk about news. Careful not to share information, especially about politics, with outsiders, Hup paints a picture of news engagement and political opinion within a close familial group:

> It's just... safer to not talk about sensitive topics with people outside my family because it would – it might – very probably lead to a disagreement, perhaps, and I want to avoid that so... at least, within the family, if you fight, you fight and then you get over it and you're still happy. So, I just feel more comfortable sharing, you know, my opinions on certain topics that, I suppose, are a bit inflammable, only within my family.

Hup's experience is typical for millennials living in multi-generational households in our study, underscoring the significance of contemporary family structures to news engagement.

As Willems (2020: 4) points out 'affordances are not independent from their environment'. This means that the platform affordances of news and related social media are not only understood within the platform itself (e.g. the mode of engagement), but are also part of the familial and social context (e.g. the meta context and consequences for news engagement). Digital media is part of a 'wider infrastructural, spatial and temporal context in which social media afford their uses' (Willems 2020: 2). For Willems, it is important to move away from platform-centrism to see how different media devices have both technological and relational affordances. 'Instead of treating mobile devices and social media platforms as separate (physical or digital) objects which function independently from the environments in which they are located', attention to relational affordances highlights how 'physical, mediated and political contexts shape the way in which mobile social media are used' (Willems: 2020: 15).

We can apply relational affordances to news engagement. The political, social, and *material and familial* context shapes news relations. A mobile device, television, radio or newspaper, are objects which rely on the technical infrastructure of cables, newspaper subscription, and monthly fees for access to digital platforms and Wi-Fi, all of which are usually shared costs within a household. Typically, parents pay for subscription fees and basic devices, and siblings pay for their monthly mobile costs and extra entertainment platforms, often with a group payment plan. Mobile social media news, by far the most common means of news for our audience members, can be reliant on these familial payment plans and shared infrastructure costs.

To go into some detail for the Malaysian digital communications infrastructures, the economic relations for news media underscore social differences for access to mixed modes of mainstream and alternative news. An urban Malaysian aged between 20–30 years old earns an average of 2000 MYR (411 EUR) per month, more than double for rural incomes in the same age range (World Bank 2020a). The cost of a monthly digital communications package (access to internet, cable channels, subscription streaming platforms and so on) is not a cost undertaken without some kind of shared economies. To have fibre internet access at home, with several members of the family living together, costs around $150–190 MYR for fibre internet (with 300 Mbps download speeds). Basic cable starts at $60 MYR a month, and with live sports coverage climbs to $90 MYR. If we add in proprietary streaming platforms and Netflix then the cost rises to $130 MYR, and if we add premium access (for four devices) then this figure rises further still, by an extra $55 MYR. In sum, to have high speed fibre internet, with basic cable and streaming platforms costs around $340 MYR (70 EUR). Whilst the average fee for monthly internet access is relatively low in Vietnam, around 257 VND (10 Euros), other cable and platform subscriptions add onto these costs (World Bank 2020b, 2020c).

This material context of sharing digital resources serves to underscore the economic relations and social bonds formed around news in the home. Older and newer modes of news from traditional devices like the television, to mobile social media, come to millennial Malaysian and Vietnamese morning, noon and evening. Making sense of these different modes of news is not something that audiences in our study do alone. Although the social affordances of the platforms could be used for public discussion, audience members mainly choose not to share and discuss news outside a tight-knit group. Parents and siblings share opinions on sensitive topics in the physical place in the home and in digital spaces where 'aunties WhatsApp groups', or friends' news groups, also serve as trusted sites for news engagement.

The family structure for Chinese Malaysian and Vietnamese millennials is dependent on a Confucian tradition of filial piety that places value on deference, respect for elders and communality rather than individuality (S.A. Tan et al 2021; Thomas, 1990). There are shifting norms for this family structure in the urban settings for our audiences, and in changing parental roles, e.g. the mother as carer and father as head of the household. Some of our audience members learned about how to check and recheck the news through their fathers, who taught them the value of news literacy, others learned through education and work experience. The family dynamics for news engagement is shifting with mobile social media: 'I don't know how to explain it, I feel like my parents are feeling younger... it's like they return to their teenage time, they are really interested in entertainment news. They know all the top stories' (30-year-old Vietnamese male graphic designer). For this audience member, parents treat national news as entertainment, increasingly relying on information from 'unofficial channels or media that try to frame their opinions. And they believe it'.

Hup, who we heard from before, commented: 'there's been a lot of fear-mongering regarding the coronavirus vaccines. You have all sorts of weird articles... unverified news sources just spreading like wildfire on WhatsApp. It's easy because people just forward it and forward it and forward it'. Hup noted how unverified news articles are spread within their 'huge family chat group', a good example of the relational affordances of mobile social media news. Sometimes they get involved: 'alright, guys, you got it wrong and it's dangerous if you believe this'. Similarly, a 28-year-old female PR consultant, living in the Greater Kuala Lumpur area, commented on 'all those aunties, uncles' who 'forward whatever news or messages that have been forwarded to them'. With these messages there comes a familial duty to counter disinformation. This 33-year-old Malaysian male analyst reflected on his role as news verifier in family news groups:

> it's come to a point where my mom and dad just put it in the family chat and tag me: 'please find out if this is true.' ... you know what happens in these auntie groups, they go all out. Yeah, since they trust me enough to let me do this, I will take it as an honor.

Jia is a 31-year-old female assistant brand manager, living in Petaling Jaya, who regularly reads *The Star, Malaysiakini, Bernama, CNN, The New York Times* and *The Guardian*, and checks news on Twitter, Outlook, Google and Facebook. The relational affordances of mobile social media news are causing some trouble in the family. Jia developed a less confrontational way of talking about news verification and rumour refutation. She explained how she handled the vexed topic of vaccinations in their aunties' and uncles' WhatsApp news groups:

> In my family, my parents' age, they do have a lot of alternative news, especially those WhatsApp messages they get and then they do believe in them... I realized for me to get through to them, it's not by just telling because they will feel that embarrassment that 'you are actually belittling me' and 'you're not listening to me', 'you have no respect towards me' and that's why they will not listen to your points. By just... calming myself down and listening to what they do say about it... a few minutes later, you're like, 'oh, I see. That's right but do you know what I heard recently?'

Jia imagines WhatsApp as Trump news, referring to the former president of the United States of America, reality TV star and property magnate: 'when I think about all these news that got forwarded so many times that you can't actually tell the actual source of it, I think about Donald Trump'. And this mode of news is targeting her parents' generation, 'less tech savvy and they are a bit out of the loop'. She explains how her parents' 'friendship circle also became a lot smaller and that's why they get a lot of their information and opinion from the friends that they trust'. Aunties ('mak cik' in Malay) share unverified sources in WhatsApp family groups. Jia takes a moment to stay calm, and then responds 'O.K. thank you to your mak cik but let's see if it's true or not'. Still, it's stressful to be the voice that verifies news: 'it's a lot tougher to verify the source if it's hearsay from family. They are so comfortable that, like, they say "who needs a source anyway? I am the source". God, no…'.

Lau Bo, a female event manager, is 30 years old and living alone in a city in southern Vietnam. Previously she worked in communications and learned 'that the news was not based on truths… the official news channels are irresponsible'. As for political news: 'in Vietnam it is like a press release from the government'. Her criticisms relate to the current Media Law (2016) which tasks the press with both the provision of truthful information and the propaganda of the policies of the Party. Citing the example of the Formosa Plastics plant and leakage of industrial pollution on the coastline (in 2016), she noted how Vietnamese news agencies 'didn't publish the negative impact of Formosa pollution, you can only read this information from international news channels or blogs and activists'. She really cares about news: 'collecting news is my interest. I love reading!' and at the same time she worries about news verification:

> It's hard to fact check news. Even for our internal news group. Everyone has different sources of information about one issue, so nothing is qualified or credible. It's just about your way of thinking or analyzing news and what you choose to believe.

Note her reference to an 'internal news group'.

Close friends share a critical mode of engagement with news, mixing different sources, checking facts and refuting rumours together. For example, a 34-year-old female agricultural supplies company director,[3] living in the Greater Kuala Lumpur area, shares news with her four friends in a WhatsApp group:

> if I share something with my friends, it's probably something that they are all passionate about so we could all discuss more about it and, perhaps, sound our opinions about all this stuff… I don't talk to people much… unless they are very close to me

The value of friends comes through clearly when audiences want to be critical of news: 'that's one way to fact check, friends have high credibility so they will tell you the truth' (30-year-old Vietnamese male graphic designer).

The modalities of news across different platforms within the home is a rich topic and outside the scope of this chapter, but it is worth pointing out family rituals can engender news engagement, particularly around memes and other non-mainstream news topics. For example, the Vietnamese lunar new year, Tet, is a time of family festivities, spiritual rituals and the possibility of renewal. It is also a time for news media that goes against the grain of traditional news, e.g. non-mainstream news reports, television satire or political memes. These alternative modes of news are a form of social resilience, from within the journalism profession and within the peripheries of mainstream media, e.g. key opinion leaders, bloggers and activists, or amateur media producers. The various ways in which Vietnamese citizens engage with news during the family ritual of lunar new year is a timely example of social resilience, a reshaping of news engagement. As families come together at this annual event, news circulates on mobile social media, sparking family talk about social issues and political culture.

In sum, the modalities of news engagement (e.g. being critical of news, checking national and international news, or verifying sources) are very much a part of familial structures and friendship groups in Malaysia and Vietnam. In terms of the relational affordances for digital media (Willems 2020), we find the physical place of inter-generational households, the mediated spaces of mobile social media, and the political and legislative context of news, act as powerful forces in shaping news engagement. In particular, familial structures shape affective encounters with news. Growing up in households where news is a daily routine, where questioning the facts and checking for bias is a normal part of news practices, our audience members carry through these critical modes of engagement for their news habits today. The mixing of older and newer modes of news (from nightly television news by official channels, to news via Twitter, Instagram and TikTok) takes place on a daily basis as different generations live together and merge older and newer types of news in one household. This mixed mode for news engagement is not without tension in the family WhatsApp news groups. Indeed, mobile social media news comes with a health warning. Our audience members look on in dismay as they see the familiar label of 'forwarded many times' in these familial news groups, feeling a filial responsibility to step in, question sources and refute rumours.

The affordances of news as it is engaged through broadcast and mobile social media are strongly relational, pointing to the 'always already' socialities of news in the home, something long associated with early audience studies of family television and radio. The dynamics of news relations highlight the 'context of context' (Dawes and Lenormand 2020) for engagement: memories of growing up with news tell us about familial contexts; collective social experiences of caution for verifying information or talking about news and opinion, tell us about political contexts. It is no wonder, then, that in a climate of distrust, the family offers a physical and emotional place of trust to discuss news and other matters, and that these 'huge WhatsApp groups' generate debate, sound discord, and, at times, spark family spats.

REFLECTIONS

In writing on citizens avoiding politics in North America, Eliasoph (1997: 605) comments on how 'penetrating this pervasive culture of political avoidance requires a new way of understanding this thing that sounds like apathy and self-interest'. We started out studying news engagement and what we found was a negation of news from audiences: at the outset people in the interviews were making negative comments about themselves ('don't read much news'), marking their disinterest in political news ('don't talk about politics') and signalling their distrust in information circulated through news and social media ('take it with a pinch of salt'). We found a pervasive culture of negation, avoiding naming things or circling around sensitive topics rather than addressing something head on. This negation signals a degree of dysfunction in how news relations work in practice.

For example, a 26-year-old Vietnamese male, working in the business sector, questioned the family news practices in their household: 'to be honest, I have a prejudice towards the Vietnamese tradition'. His father engages in the news, his mother does not: 'she is typical Vietnamese... a good kid who just follows what parents or teachers tell her to do'. His mother tells him 'we don't have to care, it's the government's business'. He rails against these norms: 'I am furious about this mindset, especially from a person who raised me'. Reflecting on his past and a culture of news disengagement ('that was my childhood, reading or not reading the news is not important'), he decided to form new patterns of news engagement, mainly through mobile social media. And yet, old habits are hard to leave behind: although they engage with news, they do so silently – 'I don't usually discuss news'. At home, he notices his father 'interested in news, but because of the environment in Vietnam, 'you know that... it's dangerous to discuss something, so we just read news to update the situation, no discussion. Sometimes I look at my dad's screen, I know he cares about the news but he never discusses'. The image of father and son silently engaging with news but avoiding talking about politics is suggestive of a pervasive culture of negation. Words like 'furious' tell us about a strong emotional reaction to norms of disengagement with news and politics passed on through generations; words like 'dangerous' tell us about negative repercussions for civic engagement; words like 'care' tell us that despite long standing practices of not knowing, people want to know more.

One of the ways of understanding 'this thing' that might sound like news avoidance, or political apathy, is through the affective modalities of media engagement. We designed the audience interviews to bring to the fore affect in the shaping of news. Political and news avoidance can be understood within an affective climate of distrust in the news and hope and despair for developing democracy. Control of news and information by the current governments in Vietnam and Malaysia mean audiences in our study have developed, over a long period, in subtly different ways, feelings of despair for public knowledge as presented in mainstream news. When speaking with a Malaysian (33-year-old male) covering political news, this participant reflected on the barriers they encountered as a journalist in gathering information, where:

> you have to ask it from the minister and hope they have the time
> for you... It's not like, in certain places, you can file a freedom of

> information request and you get everything you need. Even on the
> government's open data website, it's kind of sad.

As this Malaysian female writer succinctly put it: 'Sad. You feel sad'.

Staying with the Malaysian context, audience members looked back in anger at the absence of truth, or reliable facts, in the news, tracing their distrust and disengagement with mainstream journalism to key moments in their development as young adult citizens. For example, Jia, a brand manager (31-year-old female), grew up reading *The Star*, and now engages with mixed modes of mainstream and non-mainstream news online and through social media. She recalls the moment of realisation that news was not about facts but political narratives: 'when you found out there are these narratives, the very idealistic part of me is quite angry and then I felt the passion of doing what's right and getting the best news'. She channelled her anger and idealism into political participation, joining Berish rallies for electoral reform. And then 'the Sheraton incident, that kind of killed the spirit'. The 'Sheraton Move' is a colloquial name for events during 2020 concerning the formation and installation of the Perikatan Nasional ('National Alliance' in English) government without a general election. That anger and idealism, energised by political engagement, was replaced by 'helplessness':

> I felt like... as Malaysians, we are a bit too used to that feeling... at the
> same time, it's not that we're giving up, it's just that we have to be
> aware so that we know when to pick our fights.

Political context shapes engagement with news, both firing up citizen action and dampening the will to protest for political reform.

To return to *Milkman*, by Anna Burns, we find in the above examples echoes of the narrator in the novel reflecting on 'concentric oppressions' and the ways people 'police their own inner and outer lives' (O'Connell 2018: 1). The motif of sunsets is used by the narrator to suggest negative feelings associated with symbols of hope. For example, a teacher in a French night class, asks their students to look closely at the nightsky and see the sunset in all its variation of colours, but the students instinctively see the sunset as one colour – blue.

In another example, the narrator reflects on her maybe boyfriend's suggestion to go for a drive and look at the sunset:

> What if we accept these points of light, their translucence, their brightness; what if we let ourselves enjoy this, stop fearing it, get used to it; what if we come to believe in it, to expect it, to be impressed upon by it; what if we take hope and forgo our ancient heritage and instead, and infused, begin to entrain with it, with ourselves then to radiate it; what if we do that, get educated up to that, and then, just like that, the light goes off or is snatched away?
>
> (Burns 2018: 90)

As O'Connell notes (2018: 1), the narrator is 'channeling the Greek chorus of the community, in its conviction that to live fully is to court the possibility of loss'.

Zii is a 33-year-old male analyst working for an NGO for nature conservation. He intensely engages with different mainstream and non-mainstream news, from *Malaysiakini*, *The Edge*, *The Star*, *The Malaysian Insight*, *New Straits Times, Sarawak Report*, *Malay Mail*, as well as international news. One of the few people in our study who both discussed news in family WhatsApp groups and in comment sections on Facebook, considered themselves as motivated to engage with news in order to enhance civic debate: 'just because there is a silent majority doesn't mean that whatever you're putting out there isn't being read or being considered by somebody else... I think it's important you find ways to say things in public'. Zii knows that online debates often involve 'cyber troopers' (paid users promoting party ideology), and this provokes anger in these digital spaces. By being part of these public debates:

> you know that people are at least having a stake. They care enough to find out and they care enough to share, care enough to read and comment and react and, if anything, I think that is one thing that comforts me, making me feel like we are growing as a country, we are growing as a democracy.

Despite this personal motivation to engage with news and democratic debate, they recognise a pervasive culture of negation. They trace this to a society dealing with different periods of political and news censorship and protests for reform: for example the civil society Reformasi movement in the late 1990s, or the Bersih movement of recent years. A 'hopeless era' of the past is ever present in their memory: with 'people being arrested for random things, that was a pretty hopeless state, just depressing' (33-year-old Malaysian male analyst). His political mood impacts on (dis)engagement with news:

> There was some progress in media freedom... and, to see it changing back again so quickly with Perikatan Nasional coming back and also how the pandemic is being handled – we had a glimmer of hope there and, at this point, it's the same old BS, you know? You kind of disengage... I don't really want to go into too much detail because there's really no point knowing because there's really nothing much you can do about it... understanding where we are and the reality of things and not just getting angry all the time is important because I don't think I can handle being angry all the time... This is a pretty stressful conversation, bro.

The form of news, and its negation as a civic resource, is understood in the political and social context of the region, at this juncture in time. Their words of hope in the democratic potential of news engagement (that people 'care enough' to share, comment, read or react) constitutes a type of news relations that are deeply enmeshed in 'individual consciousness and social and political order' (Corner 2011: 51). And their words of despair for the reality of the current political climate ('same old BS') constitutes a break with news as they negatively experience it, battling with 'cyber troopers' spreading disinformation within a repressive social and political order ('there's really no point knowing'). Forms of knowledge constrain practices of knowing.

NOTES

1   Legislation for the Sedition Act and its amendments (1948, 1969) prohibits speech and publications disparaging the indigenous Malay population and the Islamic faith (Loh & Khoo 2002: 125); human rights groups have argued that the

legislation has been used to target journalists, activists, opposition party leaders and others (Pak, 2014; Amnesty International, 2016; Human Rights Watch, 2019).

2 The Malay saying 'katak di bawah tempurung' translates to 'the frog under the shell'. This participant mistranslates the phrase as 'the frog in the well'.

3 My thanks to Andreas Mattson for our discussions on 'lunar news' during this festival in Vietnam.

7

THE BELARUS PROTESTS

A CASE STUDY OF POLITICAL ENGAGEMENT

INTRODUCTION

It was compellingly evident to the majority of citizens in Belarus that Sviatlana Tsikhanouskaja had won the presidential election on August 9, 2020. Yet the following day, her advisors told her it would be unwise for her to remain in the country – for her safety it would be necessary for her to leave for Lithuania, where her children already were in exile; within two days she had fled. This was a very difficult decision for the 37-year-old housewife and English teacher who had so recently become a politician. Her husband Siarhej Tsikhanousky, who had been a popular political blogger and had launched his own presidential campaign in the spring, had been arrested in May, and was still in prison; later in 2021 he was sentenced in a sham trial to 18 years in prison, charged with 'organising mass unrest and inciting social hatred' (Reuters 2021a). The sitting president, Alexander Lukashenko, commonly known as 'the last dictator in Europe', had been in power 26 years (after 5 elections, of which only the first one, in 1994, had not been a cynical simulation of democracy). He had never engaged in any debate on television in all these years (Filipenko 2021), and

DOI: 10.4324/9781003179481-10

now wanted to make sure that there would be no serious challenger in this election. Also, in June he had the oppositional candidate Viktor Babaryka, a banker and IT-developer, arrested; he was condemned to 14 years in prison. In July, Valeryj Tsapkala, a well-known and respected politician and diplomat, who was also campaigning, felt compelled to flee the country (Börjel and Nydahl 2021:14).

In mid-July, Sviatlana Tsikhanouskaja had decided to register herself as a presidential candidate, to replace her imprisoned husband. Lukashenko apparently did not feel threatened by a politically inexperienced woman, and had allegedly added, with disdain, that the Belarusian constitution was not written with the idea that women should be in politics. Soon thereafter, Veranika Tsapkala, wife of Valryj Tsapkala, and Maryja Kalesnikava, who had been manager for Viktor Babaryka's campaign, joined forces with Sviatlana Tsikhanouskaja, placing her as the candidate representing a new political horizon in Belarus; this established what was to be a strong feminist component within the opposition. This is a feature that evokes the heroic role of women in the narratives about the struggles during World War II (Siegien and Siegien 2021). Their political ideal encompassed broad, progressive reforms for Belarus. They stressed unity over any personal political ambitions. There was a strong democratic sentiment here, but by no means explicitly Western-oriented. For example, in contrast to the so-called Ukrainian Revolution of Dignity in 2013–2014 (also known as the Maidan Revolution), there were almost no EU flags visible in the ensuing demonstrations in support of the trio. There was no widespread anti-Russian sentiment among the Belarusian population of 9.5 million; the political vision was one of continued national independence.

Long lines snaked through the streets of Belarus with citizens waiting to add their signatures to get the oppositional candidates on to the ballots – despite the pandemic. On election day, opposition voters had coordinated a plan to make visible their strength: voters folded their ballots not once, but twice. The ballots were visible through the transparent plexiglass boxes into which they were placed. The full boxes – with overwhelmingly double-folded ballots – were photographed and distributed among supporters over social media.

On the evening of August 9, the governmental election committee announced that Lukashenko had won the election with 80 percent of the vote, while Sviatlana Tsikhanouskaja got a mere ten percent. Immediately thereafter and for several days following, the streets and towns of Belarus were filled with angry citizens protesting that the election had obviously been stolen. The Belarus protests had begun. Over 13,000 photos of the events can be found here: www.gettyima ges.com/photos/belarus-protest. Each page contains 50–60 photos, but just a few pages will suffice to provide a general impression of the scale of both the protests and the violence by security forces. Also, the emblematic red and white colours of the demonstrators are clearly visible – colours that evoke the earlier Belarusian flag from two pre-vious periods: from a century ago during the brief independent pre-Soviet republic and during the first years of post-Soviet independence. The current flag is reminiscent of the one during the Soviet epoch.

An estimated one million people had been on the streets across the country (Sakhnin 2021). They were met by a shocking brutality from the security forces; about 7000 people were arrested (a number that increased to almost 40,000 after a year, with about a dozen dead or missing), with many being subjected to violence on the scene and in the prisons. Those released in the following days spoke of dreadful experiences, with much evidence on their bodies. Various media were to play a central role in the unfolding and furthering of these events. The opposition continues as of this writing (February 2022), even if they have had to fundamentally alter their strategies in the light of the repressive response by the regime. As Sviatlana Tsikhanouskaja says 'Belarusians weren't ready for this level of cruelty' (Roth 2021).

In this case study we again follow the set of parameters presented in Chapter 4. Not having direct contacts within Belarus, we have built our analysis making use of the work of other scholars and journalists, as well as materials made available by Belarusian citizens. In our ana-lysis of media engagement in the wake of the Belarus election protests, the general context plays an extensive role, as do media contexts. For ease of exposition, we divide context into four elements: some brief but key historical threads, the 2020 presidential election and its imme-diate aftermath, the year and a half since then and, finally, the media landscape itself. This overarching 'context of context' (Peck 2020) prefigures the remaining parameters, allowing them to readily fall into place in our analysis of engagement. We highlight also here at the outset that, as in many situations, media engagement interplays symbiotically with engagement predicated on face-to-face encounters. To ignore direct social interaction where it is pertinent is to lapse into a media-centric perspective; this leads to a misunderstanding of the media's role, as well as a misguided social analysis.

CONTEXTS

Historical Threads

The borders of Belarus have fluctuated through modern history, under the rule of various regional powers (for a political history of the region, see Snyder 2003; on the history of Belarus see Wilson 2021). It was not until the early 20th century that a collective identity, a 'national awakening', began in earnest, with the people calling themselves Belarusians, and with intellectuals and artists expressing their perceived rights to the language and culture. In 1918 an independent Belarusian Peoples Republic was established, but was in 1922 absorbed into the Soviet Union. Under the first decade the Belarusian language and culture was allowed to develop, but during the 1930s the republic felt the harsh assimilation policies of Stalin. Tens of thousands, especially amongst the intelligentsia, were imprisoned and/or executed (Eriksson 2021). With the Soviet invasion of Poland in 1939, the present borders of Belarus were largely solidified. During World War II Belarus was occupied by Nazi Germany from 1941 to 1944, who pursued a policy of genocide not only against the Jews but also against Slavs, if only somewhat less ambitious in its aims. As the theatre for much of the war on the Eastern Front, Belarus suffered enormously, with over two-thirds of its cities and towns devastated, 85 percent of its industry in ruins and 25 percent of its population dead. The collective memory of the Great Patriotic War lives on in Belarus as well as in Russia. Snyder (2011) situates Belarus in the middle of what he calls the Bloodlands – the parts of Eastern Europe profoundly ravaged by the conflict between Hitler and Stalin.

After the war, Belarus was rebuilt on an impressive scale, but with Stalin's militant policy of sovietisation, large numbers of Russians were moved into Belarus, with many occupying top governmental positions. Along with the obvious political bonds that this policy reinforced, it also had long-term consequence for the cultural and linguistic profile of the republic. The policy continued even after Stalin's death in 1953, and today Belarusian has become a minority language. Russian is used extensively, at home and in public contexts. About half the population can read and speak Belarusian, while only about 12 percent can write in it (World Atlas 2021). Lukashenko continued the process of Russification, and discrimination has grown against the use of the Belarus language; indeed, from the perspective of the regime, the use of the language has come to be associated with oppositional politics. The authorities thus often harass academics, cultural groups and those who assert the Belarusian language, seeing them as political enemies. Yet opposition was also to become prevalent among many Russian-speaking urban Belarusians.

These background threads – the difficult process of formation as a nation, the traumas from the 1930s and 1940s and the linguistic situation – have left their mark on the country and in various ways have had relevance in the course of the recent events. Also important to note is that the role of Lukashenko over the past 27 years has not been consistently negative. After the collapse of the Soviet Union, the neoliberal marketisation forced upon the economy caused profound social dislocation in Belarus, as in most post-communist societies. Lukashenko's promise to halt these developments helped him win the election that put him in power in 1994. He was quite successful with his economic reforms; with price controls and central planning (albeit a throwback to the Soviet era), he managed to turn around a dire situation. As one observer notes: Belarus's real GDP has doubled since 1990, and its manufacturing has tripled; agricultural output has increased by 37 percent (Sakhnin 2021), all of which initially accorded Lukashenko popularity. In relative terms, however, it lags far behind e.g. the Baltic States – who did not make use of a Soviet model in the post-communist era.

Sierakowski (2020) offers a recent snapshot of the country. He notes that first-time visitors encounter a modern and rather affluent country, one that is well-organised and managed, with a good education system and a strong work ethic. Moreover, it is technologically advanced (its IT sector would play an important role in the protests). It boasts fine urban transit and motorways, and is strikingly clean. The poverty rate is lower than other post-communist countries, and economic inequality is lower than in any EU country; there is very little unemployment or street crime. Even those who criticise Lukashenko acknowledge the high Belarusian standard of living. Yet it is a brutal authoritarian regime; those who emigrate do so mostly for political reasons, not economic ones. The country, especially the capital, Minsk, has many young people; they have no direct experience of the Soviet Union, but instead a good grasp of what is happening in the outside world, not least in terms of democratic values. Lukashenko, on the other hand, seems to have a mindset still very much coloured by the 1980s (when he was director of a collective farm); there is a compelling generation gap at work here; the support that Lukashenko still enjoys is largely with older, rural people.

The good economic news and impressive popularity were not to last, however. Belarus was becoming increasingly integrated into the global economy, while at the same time dependent on Russia for energy supply. When tensions with Moscow increased, Lukashenko tilted westward for energy and other imports. With the global economic downturn of the 2010s, Belarus felt its own situation falter, leading to two devaluations and declines in real income. Lukashenko expanded the public sector to reduce unemployment, but the state's resources were draining rapidly. Tough austerity measures were only marginally effective (Sakhnin 2021). It was becoming clear that discontent – economic and political – was growing, but apparently, given its capacity for repression, the regime never felt truly threatened. Yet anger was in the air, and spilled over into the historically unprecedented display of opposition when the election results were announced.

The 2020 Election and its Aftermath

The election took place during the pandemic; Lukashenko's mismanagement of this crisis inadvertently served as a prelude by strengthening civil society in ways that would prove useful after the election. He had dismissed the pandemic as a 'psychosis', prescribing vodka as a suitable medicine – leaving him and the regime discredited in the eyes of most citizens. Journalists were blocked from entering hospitals, and critical news sites were prevented from reporting on the pandemic. With no viable state-led measures to deal with COVID-19, Belarusians had to deal with it on their own. Cooperative networks were set up to buy masks and equipment, with citizens assisting medical personnel. A new solidarity emerged, as more people got to know and trust each other (Sierakowski 2020).

In the days prior to the election on August 9, the intelligence service of Belarus – that still uses the Soviet-era name of KGB – began arresting large numbers of activists and journalists, calling them 'provocateurs'. Also, on August 4, early voting of an unusually high level led to suspicions of fraud – ballot stuffing (Sean Williams 2020). Two days later Sviatlana Tsikhanouskaja called on citizens to register, using an alternative voting platform; by the next day, over a million Belarusians had signed up. This may well have triggered the regime's nervousness: the internet and landline telephones were cut, along with foreign news services such as CNN and Al Jazeera. The regime blamed 'cyberattacks' for the outage. Belarus has a highly developed IT sector, with over 100,000 people employed; makeshift substitutes emerged, but still about a quarter of the population was offline. In the ensuing chaos, Lukashenko not only pronounced himself the winner, but made sure that Sviatlanamade Tsikhanouskaja felt sufficiently threatened to leave the country. Protests began to erupt.

There was also action percolating on the media front. Telegram is a widely used social media app in Belarus, a platform hosting dozens of channels to which Belarusians subscribe. It was slowed during the outage, but oppositional IT experts had it running again, albeit in a reduced capacity, on the evening of August 10. Telegram almost immediately became the main source of non-official news in the country. The most popular channel was NEXTA Live, ('nexta' means 'someone' in Belarusian) first launched as a YouTube channel in 2015. It was run by Stsiapan Putsila an oppositional activist living in exile in Poland, and Roman Protasevich (who was arrested 21 May 2021 after Belarusian warplanes forced the Ryanair passenger plane he was on to land in Minsk). NEXTA Live had already gained about 1.3 million followers at the time of the election; with the election and media blackout this figure now rose sharply to over two million (Sean Williams 2020; Sjparaga 2021). NEXTA Live was making available practical information like maps of police locations, addresses where protesters could hide, contacts for lawyers and human rights groups, as well as instructional resources like how to set up web proxies. It was also sharing images of police brutality. Telegram, with channels that could provide information useful for self-organisation even at the level of apartment blocks (Gerdžiūnas 2020), and NEXTA Live in particular, played a major role in developing social connectivity; people realised they were not alone (Sean Williams 2020).

On August 14, Sviatlana Tsikhanouskaja stated from her exile in Lithuania that she had received 60–70 percent of the vote, and announced the creation of a so-called 'Coordination Council' to ease a transfer of power. The Council, comprised of civil society activists and respected professionals, included Nobel Prize laureate Svetlana Alexievich and eight others. Three days later she said she was ready to lead a transitional government and organise free and fair elections. US Secretary of State Mike Pompeo expressed support for the council, as did a spokesperson for Vladimir Putin, noting that the Council had expressed no intentions of reducing relations with Russia. On September 17, the EU Parliament recognised the Council as the interim representation of the Belarusian people. Lukashenko promised 'appropriate measures' against this 'attempt to seize power', and the chief prosecutor launched criminal charges against the Council members, whom Lukashenko labelled a 'terrorist group'; ultimately all of them would either be in jail or, like Svetlana Alexievich, be forced to flee the country.

The 2020 presidential election was the first to be contested by members of Belarus' elite strata (i.e. the banker Viktor Babaryka and the diplomat Valeryj Tsapkala), as well as by a popular blogger (Siarhej Tischanousky). Lukashenko, used to thinking in terms of political leaders and established candidates, imprisoned or drove into exile such people, apparently thinking the problem was then solved (Malerius 2021). He was not prepared for a popular revolt, especially not one led by a politically inexperienced housewife in exile. The opposition, while massive, was by no means total, however; Belarusians were divided, as we discuss below in regard to motivations behind the protests.

The first days of demonstrations were met with brutal response from the security forces, especially the dreaded OMON, the dark-clad riot police with their shields and weapons, and their balaclavas to keep their identity secret. On Wednesday, August 14, a 'miracle' took place, as Sierakowski (2020) puts it. The streets became filled with women and girls all dressed in white – providing a dramatic symbolic counter-point to the dark uniforms and equipment of the security forces – and again underscoring the feminist element of the movement. Holding flowers, the women demonstrated all day; the next day they were joined by many industrial workers, followed by transit workers, who all stood with the women. The security forces became perplexed. The following day, in front of the national assembly, the women in white began embracing the security forces and decorating them with flowers. These events, with the moral paralysis of the security forces, went viral on social media.

The regime shifted tactics, and instead tried to prevent marches and demonstrations by barricading key streets and squares. Ultimately this proved futile; people continued coming out in large numbers. On August 16, a week after the election, a crowd of over 100,000 marched to the city centre. The 'March for Freedom', as demonstrators called it, became a regular Sunday event for several weeks. At the end of August, Lukashenko, in his autocratic manner, ordered the Interior Ministry and the KGB to terminate what he called the 'riots'. The vicious repression returned; the regime cleared the streets with terror, making visible protest simply too dangerous.

A Year and Half of Repression – and Response

By October the large demonstrations had subsided, and soon vanished completely; people did not dare to publicly express opposition. Yet this did not mean that engagement had evaporated; it was rather forced to find other means of expression. Sviatlana Tsikhanouskaja continued to maintain publicity for the opposition by meeting with heads of state and other officials in the West, and giving interviews in the mainstream media. Manifestations of support continued, especially from neighbouring countries, often making use of specific Belarusian symbols, such as hanging up paper airplanes to demand the release of the journalist Romain Protasevich, arrested from the downed Ryanair flight (which also resulted in international condemnation of Lukashenko, as well as sanctions). The regime, for its part, continued to maintain a tight security within the country, and relentlessly pursued Belarusian journalists and blocked foreign journalists from covering the situation as much as they could. 'Security chancellors' have been installed at universities, and new laws provide security force members with impunity from any violation of the law they might commit in their line of duty (Sjparaga 2021).

A year after the election, the repression against journalists and other civil society actors intensified. In July and August 2021, the offices and homes of many Belarusian human rights organisations and their staff were searched, including the Belarusian Association of Journalists. Documents and much technical equipment were seized. More than 30 media workers and dozens of bloggers were in prison. In July, Amnesty International reported at least 46 civil society organisations, not least the Belarusian PEN Centre and many focused on human rights, had been shut down. Activists claim the number is now approaching 100. Lukashenko, in a rather forthright statement, called these actions a 'purge' (Johnson 2021). In the course of the 12 months, according to the International Federation for Human Rights (FIDH) and Viasna, a Belarusian rights organisation, at least 35,000 peaceful demonstrators had been detained, with almost 4,700 court cases. There were also over 600 political prisoners and about 1,800 reports of torture. Hundreds of human rights activists have been persecuted and thousands of citizens have had to flee the country (Johnson 2021).

In this grim situation, engagement nonetheless continued, facilitated both by face-to-face encounters and media use. In the first post-election months, there was the development of what soon was known as 'the republic of the yards' (Strotsev 2021). Particularly in the high-rise suburbs, the courtyards are spaces mostly seen as impersonal, to be crossed quickly; they were quite uninviting. Then, on election day, people began seeing their neighbours – many of whom they recognised but did not personally know – arriving at the polling stations, with red and white colours. They understood that they were political allies; they began speaking with each other, sharing experiences and hopes. After the results of the election became known and anger rose, windows and balconies became decorated in red and white colours of the opposition, and people began gathering in the yards, talking – about suffering, indignation and resistance. Whole new networks of engagement began to take shape in Belarusian society. The discussions and chats from the courtyards of the apartment blocks began to be circulated on the Telegram app, and helped participants organise for the marches.

At first these mediated contacts played a subordinate role to the large-scale marches themselves, but as these demonstrations began to be crushed by the regime, these neighbourhoods of opposition became centres for discussions, lectures, live music of all genres, poetry, dance, theatre, art courses and programmes for children. There were hundreds of such spaces just in Minsk. The online sharing of these cultural practices – that now went far beyond just discussions – profoundly deepened engagement and the sense of solidarity. Mediated and live encounters generated reciprocal inspiration. Gradually the regime began to recognise the threat posed by this development. Security forces, including OMON and plainclothes police, as well as civil servants, began a massive campaign to clear out these 'republics'. The areas were stormed, protest symbols were removed and people in the yards as well as in their apartments, often in a random fashion, were arrested and often beaten. In one particularly militant residential area, Novaja Botovaja, the regime turned off the water and heating. But rather than having the intended effect of breaking resistance, these acts were met by solidarity from other areas in the city, providing water, food and warm clothing to the desperate residents. The yards are quiet, but red-white-red flags and graffiti still appeared – keeping the regime busy with their removal.

Among the ever-growing Belarusian diaspora there have been contributions to the opposition from abroad, not least people with expertise in digital technologies, who could offer much useful assistance. The Belarusian IT sector has long been not only technologically very advanced, but also represented an important share of the economy. Lukashenko's brutal response resulted in a serious brain-drain of such expertise, adding to the economic difficulties. Especially in Poland local organisations are working together with Belarusians in exile to assist new refugees (Chowdovnik and Marques 2021). Civil society groups in Poland with names such as The Ministry of Light Industry deals with the basic needs of the newcomers. The Ministry of Housing helps them find lodging, while The Ministry of Language assists them with learning Polish (Roth 2021). In Warsaw there is even an organisation of defectors from the police and security forces, ByPol. They carry out investigations into the regime, gathering materials and assist activists still within Belarus. They plan and organise for a future democratic transformation of Belarus.

The Belarus Free Theatre is troupe of 16 people who have since 2005 held documentary performances and workshops about the politics and culture of Belarus. At first these were clandestine arrangements within Belarus – in schools, yards, living rooms – with publicity about the events being transmitted via encoded messages. Increasingly this became too dangerous; the two founders of the group fled to London in 2011, and were eventually joined by the rest plus a number of family members. There are live shows planned for London in 2022, but most of their work is live-streamed to Belarus – theatre performances as well as courses in theatre, art, activism and journalism. They see their work as political resistance, as a way to help maintain Belarusian cultural identity. They have chosen a precarious existence, however: they do not seek asylum, for then they would not be allowed to work while their cases were being handled (Haglund 2021).

Within the world of sports, the Belarusian Sports Solidarity Foundation (BSSF) helps defend athletes, players and coaches against the regime. This became globally visible when sprinter Krystina Tsimanouskaya, who had publicly criticised her coaches on social media at the Tokyo Olympic games in August 2021 (originally scheduled for 2020, but postponed due to the pandemic). The regime began a hate campaign against her on national state television, and the coaches attempted to quiet her and whisk her away, back to Minsk. With the help of BSSF she was able to reach Poland, as was her family, and was granted asylum. The two coaches were dismissed from the Olympics Games. BSSF, who has thus far assisted about 120 sport professionals, was threatened or punished for perceived political dissent (Roth 2021).

Other forms of engagement and solidarity continue. Writing a year after the election, Olga Sjparaga (2021) observes that Belarusians write large numbers of letters to political prisoners, who in turn encourage those who are still free to maintain their spirit for struggle. Many citizens come to witness at the sham trials of peaceful protesters and to express their solidarity with them. Citizens also continue to organise for smaller, more clandestine events. According to Sjparaga (2021) a new infrastructure of mutual assistance and care has emerged, which has altered horizontal social relations within the country. Together with the impressive virtue of patience, she sees this as an immense resource for the society in its efforts to move forward democratically. Indeed, it is ironically the violence of the regime that has engendered these traits.

The Media Landscape

The fundamental fact about the pre-election media landscape in Belarus was that it was dominated by traditional media – radio, television and press – controlled by the government. There were a number of independent outlets, whose existence was always somewhat precarious, such as the weekly magazine *Nasha Niva*, Radio Svaboda and the independent internet portal TUT (Sierakowski 2020). The regime's media policy was a mix of censorship, disinformation and promotion of Lukashenko as the nation's leader, lauding him, his actions and his decisions. Like much of the way Belarusian society was organised, media policy was largely derived from the former Soviet era, with a strongly independent, nationalist spin. Also, the state had full control of incoming and outgoing internet traffic. No internet service providers (ISPs) have direct access to foreign net traffic without permission (Varna 2020). With the government having such control over traditional media, but also given the advanced character of the Belarusian IT sector and the technical infrastructure, it is perhaps not surprising that other options began to emerge, and the landscape was altered.

As the election approached, Lukashenko felt reasonably secure. He and his election team were not paying much attention to what was happening online, that various platforms and their channels had become very popular. They assumed that the regimes propaganda machinery in the traditional media would be sufficient to gain victory. The opposition, however, was relying on the newer media. The unregistered presidential candidate Siarhei Tsickanousky had become well known and popular via the YouTube channel Country for Living, and campaigned there and on the streets until he was arrested (with, as noted above, his campaign then taken over by his wife Sviatlana Tsikhanouskaja). Victor Babaryka was active on Instagram before his arrest.

As mentioned earlier, the three female leaders of the opposition began using social media to promote their campaign, to share thoughts and to maintain dialogue with supporters. They also toured the country, holding rallies that were announced online, encouraging people to join them on the streets – again highlighting the complementarity of mediated and live encounters. Their supporters in turn could share links with each other and engage in discussion. This was a profoundly new ingredient in Belarusian political culture, and served to stimulate engagement and establish online civil society bonds and civic trust between people who previously did not know each other. The three women were perceived as down to earth – a striking contrast to the traditional (male) autocratic political leaders of the older generation (Laputsla 2021).

Independent media channels and websites facilitated live streams using Instagram, Facebook and YouTube. Soon, however, there was a gradual shift to Telegram. By late 2019, the Telegram platform had become a sort of alternative public sphere of ideas, as well as a tool for oppositional organisation. This platform had already served the people well in the spring during the pandemic: with the authorities providing little or misleading information about COVID-19, people turned to Telegram to learn about the spread of the virus, the death toll and what measures to take. Leaked information and anonymous accounts of what was going on began appearing on Telegram channels – which established them as trustworthy news sources. As the political drama unfolded in Belarus, Telegram, especially the NEXTA Live channel, became the major site for ongoing updates of the developments. It also offered instructions on how to sidestep possible internet blockage – which indeed came immediately after the election.

Telegram channels were used for mutual aid, for example to obtain codes for buildings where protesters could hide, to inform where protesters could find water and medicine, to provide lists of people arrested and for the coordination of assistance for those released. Special channels served to reveal the identity of officials involved in violence for future accountability (Asmolov 2020). Further, along with general coordination in the streets, Telegram has proved to be highly useful (along with Signal and WhatsApp) in facilitating 'flash mobs' as a strategy via coordinated real time communication. (Tucker 2021).

Efforts to close down Telegram (by arresting some administrators) or to technically block it (by closing the entire national internet system down) had proved futile, much to Lukashenko's frustration. Immediately after the election, on the evening of August 9, the decision was taken to shut down the entire national internet system. It was short-lived, however, and the regime reopened the internet on August 12. Closing down the internet was a desperate measure and proved to be a costly for the economy: an estimated $56 million per day as ATMs and all internet-related services, not least financial instruments, ceased to function (Varna 2020). While the whole country essentially experienced an internet blackout, some were still able to access Telegram with the help of the tech administrators and the pre-installed open-source internet censorship circumvention devices (Varna 2020).

The regime had hoped that the shutdown would break the spirit of the opposition, but found to its consternation that once service was reinstated, the opposite happened. Now images of police brutality were going massively viral, hundreds of thousands of new subscribers joined the platform, and engagement had become re-energised, triggering more marches and even strikes in major state enterprises across the country. Government spokespeople claimed that the internet disruption derived from foreign attacks, but technical evidence conclusively shows it to have been done by the regime (Varna 2020).

With the information about the regime's violent crackdown spreading, even much of the staff of the Belarusian State Television and Radio Company went out, refusing to broadcast the lies of the regime. Lukashenko's response was to bring in journalists and commentators from Russia to fill the missing slots. Quickly the airwaves were filled with interviews with Russian hard-line supporters of Lukashenko. Belarusian state television began sending footage supplied by the video news agency Ruptly from the Russian state TV network RT. Replacement newscasters referred to Belarus as 'Belorussia', a term usually not used in Belarus, but normal in Russia (Shotter and Seddon 2021). If many Belarusians had found the propagandistic broadcasting media intolerable for its lies and censorship, insult was no doubt added to injury by this foreign presence. Belarusians by and large are not anti-Russian; it is at present difficult to say if this is now changing.

Despite the importance of Telegram, YouTube was not abandoned. Many important activists maintained their presence there. New channels were established by actors, classical musicians and singers to share their performances, after it became impossible for them to function in public. Belarusian activists began giving interviews to bloggers from Russia and Ukraine, spreading their thoughts to Russian-speaking audiences abroad. NEXTA, a co-channel of NEXTA Live, recommenced on YouTube in the autumn with live streams discussing the situation inside and outside Belarus. It also showed a documentary titled *Lukashenko: The Golden Bottom*, that deals with the autocrat's alleged corruption, his wealth and his networks.

The Telegram platform was developed by Russian IT activists Pavel Durov and his brother Nikolai as an anti-censorship tool that could circumvent blackouts and also allow its administrators to message large number of people simultaneously. It can be described as a hybrid between WhatsApp and Twitter, in that it has the capacity for one-on-one or group encrypted chats (as well as voice and video calls), but also allows for one-to-many communication through its array of channels that users can follow in a manner very similar to following accounts on Twitter. Telegram, importantly, has fine privacy functions, including a particularly secure 'secret chat' function (Shotter and Seddon 2021).

Stsiapan Putsila, the young co-founder of NEXTA Live, had some years earlier at the age of 17 set up a YouTube channel for music videos – often of a political nature that taunted the regime and Lukashenko in particular. When he began putting up videos of current affairs, his viewership grew, and his channel was soon blocked. A criminal case was initiated for insulting the president. He relocated to Warsaw, saw the possibilities of Telegram, and with some friends launched the channels NEXTA and NEXTA Live on Telegram (Shotter and Seddon 2021), where he soon gained a reputation for challenging the narratives of the regime.

In coordinating marches and other manifestations, Putsila says decisions were taken by a group of 15 people, including activists and media administrators, not by himself alone. There has been some criticism that he and the channels blur the boundaries between activism and journalism. This he does not deny, but defends himself by saying that in the media circumstances just after the election, he felt there was no other alternative, and the protesters had in fact asked for his assistance (Shotter and Seddon 2021). From the perspective of classic liberal journalism there have certainly been problems with NEXTA Live and other channels. Also, observers note that risks for disinformation are always present; for example, the regime has attempted, apparently without too much success, to use anonymous Telegram channels for disinformation and provocation (Asmolov 2020). These channels were sharing thousands of images and videos each day, as well as leaked documents and other materials. Despite efforts to cross-reference materials, and the use of geolocating to confirm sources, without the resources of a large staff to fact-check and do suitable editing – and with a great reliance on anonymous sources – mistakes will inevitably seep in. Having to both cover and guide the protests has been an enormous responsibility (Gerdžiūnas 2020), and it is hard to claim the Telegram channels could or should have done anything differently.

MOTIVATIONS BEHIND THE PROTESTS

In looking at the motivations behind the engagement manifested in the protests, there is certainly something obvious at work. Many people reacted with indignation and anger when it became clear that the official election results were fraudulent. As they went out to demonstrate peacefully, they were met with violent repression; they experienced a savagery by the security forces in the streets – with beatings and tear gas, as well as in the prisons, with very cruel treatment, including torture. Soon a number of deaths were recorded. This was plenty enough to mobilise a collective opposition, one that would spur hundreds of thousands of people not only to join further marches, but also to organise, to generate new social networks, to develop new forms of cooperation – to confront the regime.

Yet there is more. Looking at the history, discontent had been growing for a number of years prior to the 2020 election due to the economic downturn the country experienced. While this on its own is not at all likely to have set of such a profound response, the character of Lukashenko's regime, and not least his autocratic manner of handling difficulties, had no doubt alienated him from many citizens. Large sectors of the public felt little sympathy for him; they were not prepared to give him any slack. He was no 'friend', even if he was respected for the impressive economic development he had come to oversee in his first years in power.

Lukashenko, who appears to have near-total control over Belarus, was also a man whose horizons appear to be rather insular and have been frozen in time, while many of the younger, educated urban population had been able to follow what was happening in the outside world. Despite the restrictions on the media, they were steadily gaining impressions from abroad, following cultural trends, knowledge development (not least within IT), and political values in regard to democracy, freedom and dignity. This did not appear to be framed by a strict East-West perception – as we noted, there was no strong clamouring to join EU, nor was there any significant anti-Russian expression. One might call it – with due modesty – a process of enlightenment applied to themselves as a nation, as people. While grateful for the post-independence economic growth, many citizens, through the media they could access, were developing horizons that exceeded the contemporary realities of Belarus.

Travel played no doubt an important role as well – even if Belarusians with normal passports were not permitted to travel to Western countries, with the exception of a few in Latin America. Various members of the elite (businessmen, officials, etc.) have had more liberty – and no doubt many of them had come to reinterpret the situation in their own country. As understanding of the outside world grew, one can guess that these restrictions in themselves became a source of frustration and irritation. In June of 2021, there came a temporary ban on travel abroad for most Belarusians; the official explanation was that this was a measure against the COVID-19 pandemic, but many saw it as a way to prevent more people from leaving the country.

We would also suggest that the new forms of mutual assistance that emerged also expressed and further facilitated motivation. The cloud of anonymity that had hovered over Belarusian society began to dissipate as citizens built up networks, joined marches together, had discussions and cultural events in the courtyards. A new sense of 'we' emerged – and continues. One could argue, as Eriksson (2021) does, that it this represents a form of 'national rebirth', a new sense of shared identity, where the citizens seemingly had transformed themselves from being the objects of historical forces to being the subjects of their fate. Those who could look further back in history of Belarus could well insist that this was unprecedented. Thus, we would say that the subjective dispositions behind the motivations at its most basic was driven by a moral repugnance against the regime's handling of the election and its aftermath, but was enhanced by a growing insight into the discrepancies between the political realities of Belarus and more attractive versions inspired from abroad, as well as by the new sense of collective self-empowerment.

Yet we must keep in mind that Belarusians were divided; not everyone supported the protests. The profile of the demonstrators was mixed; 20 percent were between 18 and 29 years of age, another 20 percent over 55. It was decidedly not just a youth movement. The protesters tended to be better educated, urban, Russian-speaking, with many professionals and cultural occupations represented ('the creative precariat'), along with many IT specialists. The educated, creative precariat is especially interesting, in that many are freelancers connected to global media markets or ad hoc internationally networked projects focused on human rights, environment, gender issues and so on. In other words, a resourceful, competent and globally aware strata (Gapova 2021).

Somewhat surprisingly – and happily, from the protesters' point of view – a good number of industrial workers also joined the opposition, comprising about a fifth of the activists in the first few weeks. This was notable not least because most industry is state-owned, continuing the Soviet model, with high job security and attractive benefits. Volodymyr (2021) suggests that the very general, non-ideological and non-work related character of the protesters' demands helped facilitate this allegiance – as well as the brutality they saw inflicted on many of their own colleagues by the police when they first began voicing opposition. Thus, they too experienced a new collective subjectivity, of solidarity. It was soon squelched, however, by the threats of dismissals and the fear of remaining jobless for the rest of their lives. In the process, the regime managed also to crush the last independent labour unions (Winiarski 2021).

An important feature of Belarusian society to understand here is that there exists a quasi-class divide between those 'inside' and those 'outside' the prevailing system (Gapova 2021). Those on the inside are employed by the state, tend to receive good benefits and are generally secure. The higher-ups on the inside – high-ranking bureaucrats, state prosecutors and so on, wield much power, as do businessmen on the inside. Outsiders – even those with wealth – are always more vulnerable – the creative precariat being a prime case in point.

A study done by Centre for East European and International Studies (ZOiS) in December 2020, that is, four months into the revolt, found that 29 percent of the citizens supported the protests fully, 16 percent partially. About one third were against the protests – a figure that would be higher if people in rural areas and senior citizens had been included. From another angle it emerges from the results that about 20 percent of the population are solid 'silent loyalists' to the regime, and about 25 percent are 'silent opponents' who did not dare participate. Another 20 percent expressed a disinterest in politics altogether. Clearly, however, there was much support for the mobilisation, even if a sizeable part of the population did not align themselves with it. Of the 2000 Belarusians sampled in December 2020, 14 percent said they had participated in the protests, but 6 percent declined to answer that question – probably out of safety concerns. A full 20 percent said that they or people they know had suffered violence during the protests (Krawatzek and Sasse 2021). The picture these figures offer is of course only a snapshot, and attitudes no doubt evolved over time.

Thus, we see patterns in the extent and character of motivation. One's position in regard to the system tended to have much bearing on how one perceived the protests; the loyalty of the military and police, e.g., remained largely intact, despite some defections of unknown numbers. Those within the system felt less motivated to support the protests; these groups no doubt felt they had much to lose by a radical transformation of society. Older rural populations, following patterns established in many other countries, also felt less motivated to support change. Urban dwellers, the more educated felt more motivation for a democratic transition, as did younger people and the cultural workers, many of whom were strongly oriented to the outside world. Likewise, most of the IT sector had global horizons that strengthen their motivation to see a democratic dawn in Belarus.

And finally, not surprisingly, a significant number of people were reluctant to express their views at all in the face of such a brutally repressive regime.

MODALITIES OF MEDIA PRACTICES AND TACTICS

In protest movements people have instrumental goals – there are important things that they want to change. Thus, there is a strategic, cognitive modality to protest. But alongside this instrumental stance there is also an important affective, expressive modality – one that connects with people's subjectivity, to shape collective identity and foster a sense of belonging, of a shared struggle. It aims at influencing public opinion via affective appeals, not just rational argument, engaging new recruits, and messaging to the broader society and to the world the values of the movement – of course in hopes of gaining support. Both communicational modalities have been prominent in the Belarus protests.

On the cognitive, instrumental side there has been the vast flow of alternative news and information, as an antidote to the official journalism of the regime. This has been vital for the protesters – to have a firm, realistic grasp of what is happening in the country (as well as abroad, e.g. in gaining support). The protesters' social media platforms illustrate this need very well. Further, as a means of organising and coordinating the various activities of the movement, strategy and tactics necessitate instrumental information – often very much in the moment, e.g. during a demonstration – to know where the security forces are mobilising, which streets are safe and so on.

The affective modality is more subtle. It involves building collective identities among a population that is sociologically not homogeneous, generating symbols, mobilising rhetoric and appealing to historical memory in ways that will speak to as many (diverse) groups as possible – and thus engage them. In a crisis situation such as in Belarus after the 2020 election, it is important to try to empower as many people as possible through affective communication, one that can create a new, engaging imaginary. The protesters manifested impressive creativity in this regard; their aim was to promote a pluralist civic identity that many could relate to, going beyond the narrower ethnocultural identity of earlier protests in Belarus (Gabowitsch 2021).

It was clear from the beginning that the protest movement was aiming for broad unity and avoiding ideological positioning. This was motivated not least by the wide variety of the groups who joined the movement – medical professions, IT experts, business people, academics, students, workers, pensioners. This infused a rich diversity of creative input to the movement, yet they could settle on three key demands: free election, the release of political prisoners and an end to state violence. In essence, only die-hard supporters of the regime would find these demands unacceptable. It is noteworthy that the three original female figures fronting the movement in the immediate aftermath of the election spoke to crowds in the second- and third voice: 'We are incredible!' soon became 'Belarusians – you are great!' These three figures were quickly removed from the scene by the authorities, but the movement was not predicated on rallying around a leader – it had a strong horizontal character. Slogans in the crowd such as 'Stop the violence!' invite a civic community to collectively give voice to the common good (Gabowitsch 2021).

The marches often had a compelling performative dimension – theatre, music, song, slogans – that could generate subjective response; the size of the crowds themselves could serve as an invitation to join. Large flags and banners were visible, with the red-white-red colours of the opposition. These were mostly produced collectively by the protesters, reflecting a solidarity of shared labour. During the marches themselves, but particularly in the courtyards and spaces between buildings in urban areas, people were getting to know each other in an unprecedented manner; new bonds were being established through conversation, song, music, poetry and mutual aid. This connectivity began engendering a new regime of subjectivity in Belarus (Lewis 2021), to which the authorities unsurprisingly responded forcefully. Yet the emotion of fear can also be channelled into resistance, and strengthen bonds between people.

Collective identity is of course a fundamental element in any society, and since its independence, identity politics in Belarus has followed two different paths. The official version promoted the achievements of the Soviet period, the building of the socialist republic, and the heroic struggle against the Nazis in the Great Patriotic War, the post-war reconstruction, and the success in new era of independence (Bekus 2021). Oppositional discourses since the late 1980s have been less unified; they have promoted conservative ethno-nationalism, anti-communism, democracy and modernism. In this mix the suffering under Stalinism and later Soviet rule had a prominent role – though it never challenged the primacy of World War II as a national calamity. The 2020 protests mostly avoided the tension embedded in these two narratives, by appropriating and recasting some of the old symbolism as well as creating new ones that could provide alternative frames of understanding.

For example, the red-white-red flag, originally from the brief independent republic of a century ago, was also used in the first years of independence after the breakup of the Soviet Union. When Lukashenko came to power, he replaced it with a green and red flag that evoked the one from the Belarusian the Soviet republic. Red and white now took on a new meaning. These colours signalled the new, democratic post-Lukashenko Belarus (but were also seen by the regime as an anti-Russian stance). The red and white colours on flags, banners, pennants, were also sprayed on walls, taped up on paper on lamp posts, visible on clothing; they became ubiquitous. The regime recognised the power of these symbols to inspire, and not only frantically removed such displays as quickly as they could, but also began arresting anyone wearing these colours. Many people on marches carried red and white umbrellas – perhaps echoing solidarity with the umbrella movement in the Hong Kong protests (Fung 2020). The umbrellas had a practical use as well: they could help protect the demonstrators from the dye in the water cannons used by the regime to identify participants even after the marches (Bekus 2021).

In other settings protesters made use of both the memory of the war against the Nazis – some online messages would call for people to marches or meetings addressing them as 'partisans', evoking the heroic fighters who helped defeat fascism, or speak of the 'the Motherland', an appellation from the same period. Alternatively, there would be convocations for the victims of Stalinism, thereby associating the current regime with the atrocities from the 1930s – a powerful motif. Thus, both modalities were at work, neatly complementing each other.

INTENSITIES OF ENGAGEMENT

The protests manifested a profoundly intense engagement; they had in essence launched a non-violent revolution, and were being met by brutal repression, which in turn at first only served to deepen the intensity of their commitment. This intensity carried the protesters through much adversity, and also energised the building of large social networks, online and in the neighbourhoods. It helped generate many creative measures for the protesters to take, of both instrumental and expressive modalities. As the repression continued and escalated, however, it became clear that street demonstrations had become too risky; this high level of intensity, with constant mobilisations and behind the scenes work with the online media, could not be sustained. Thus ended the first phase of the protests. Other, more clandestine ways were found to maintain engagement, e.g. through mutual help that could proceed under the radar of the regime, though this of course signalled a new phase, with a reduced level of intensity.

While intensity is mostly conceived as an emotional phenomenon, it can also be manifested in moral terms – that engagement can be driven by a normative vision, an ethical horizon that propels it forward. This was certainly the case with the first collective moral revulsion over the election fraud – a breach of fundamental principles that demanded rectification. It was also visible in the efforts of protesters to 'unmask' – figuratively and metaphorically – the security forces of their balaclavas or helmet masks – with an eye to morally shame them in front of the nation, and hopefully, to hold them accountable in some future judicial process. The effect was often that the individual tried to cover his face and withdrew from the confrontation. Some demonstrators would not only attempt to tear off the masks to reveal the faces, but also take photos and put them up on one of the Telegram channels. In particular a channel called 'The Black Book of Belarus' was devoted to 'de-anonymising' the police and security forces. From a photo, the activists at this channel would use facial recognition technology. If this was not successful, they would put the photo out on the channel and ask if anyone could recognise the individual, hoping to get the name. With that they could gather other information and put the full identity on the channel (Walker 2020). The regime quickly began arresting anyone suspected of such activities, but the point here is the moral intensity behind these practices – a strong sense that these people should not be allowed to commit such violence with impunity.

CONSEQUENCES

A year and a half after the protests began against the fraudulent election, the most obvious consequence is that the opposition movement was crushed, at least in its public manifestations. It did not achieve its goals of free elections, an end to political violence and the release of political prisoners. Indeed, by now some 40,000 have been arrested, many are still in prison, and thousands of Belarusians have gone into exile. Lukashenko is still in power, as autocratic as ever. There has been much debate about the strategy of the protest movement. Some, such as Sakhnin (2021), and Siegien and Siegien (2021) claim that the fundamental problem was that protesters offered no clear political programme, and expressed only vague visions of a post-Lukashenko Belarus. Most political observers submit, however, that any such steps toward a more specific political ideology would have split the movement. The time was not ripe for such politics; in that moment of crisis, gaining as much unity in support of the movement was crucial (Sjparaga 2021).

Yet, in this defeat there are some important gains for a possible democratic Belarus in the future. For one, the difficult struggles united a large segment of the population, provided them with a collective 'we' as subjects who dared to attempt to make their own history. Innumerable new social relations and contacts have been established, new networks of solidarity have been generated. Much of the earlier anonymity of the society has been superseded. There is a new, rich 'civic capital' hovering under the surface of the still-repressed society. Moreover, they have gained massive amounts of practical experience, in organising not just protests, but also cultural events in the courtyards, in the use of digital technologies, in how to deal with a repressive apparatus. The mutual support, both within and from abroad, continues; spirits are not broken, despite the high price many have had to pay. The level of preparedness today should a new opportunity for a new liberatory uprising present itself is immensely more developed than it was in the summer of 2020.

There have been consequences in the global arena. Lukashenko has become an international pariah; his is viewed as a gangster state, and many sanctions and restrictive measures have been passed by the international community – even if these will cause economic stress for many citizens. His position has become increasingly difficult, with the result that he has sought help from Russia's Vladimir Putin. The irony is that Lukashenko long tried to avoid such dependency; now Belarus risks becoming a vassal state of Russia – all because he so desperately held on to his personal power. As often is the case, political movements can have unanticipated and unintended consequences. The future will tell how the present developments resolve themselves for the people of Belarus.

For our purposes, this case study demonstrates the analytic utility of the engagement parameters. The context, however, is seemingly atypical – most discussions of democracy do not address repressive regimes in any detail. Yet, in a global perspective, we would do well to recall that only about 15 percent of the world's population live in liberal democracies (the statistics vary, depending on the definitional criteria used; our source, Roser and Herre 2022, is among the more generous). The vast majority live in limited or 'weak' democracies, or in elected or closed autocracies. While degrees of freedom and repression vary, so do the modes of response and depth of resistance (as illustrated, e.g. in the cases of Malaysia and Vietnam): power relations, resources and engagement always differ in every situation. The extreme character of the circumstances in Belarus is thus a factor of degree, not of kind – and in fact serves to highlight the role of especially context in regard to engagement: here, as often is the case, it is multi-dimensional.

***

NB: Names are spelled differently in the Russian and Belarusian languages; moreover, translations vary, both in English and Swedish. We have chosen what we perceive to be the most common renditions in English, and have remained consistent with them in the text.

8

CONCLUSION

CONTINGENCIES OF MEDIA ENGAGEMENT

To be engaged with the media means more than being taken up with, diverted by, or reactive to social media, a cultural artefact or event. Engaging with the media, in the context of politics, society and culture is a significant psychological investment in something or someone that matters in that moment and, or, over a longer period of time. Moreover, we treat the real significance of engagement as collective phenomena, rather than just as individual significance. This is why engagement matters; it tells us about the connections across reason and rationality, affect and emotion, and why groups of people connect or disconnect with political and popular culture.

Our argument about engagement as a nexus of relations (see Figure 8.1) draws upon various scholarly research within political and social theory, media and cultural studies, which sees engagement 'within a larger range of psychological orientations to the world and to the artefacts within it' (Corner 2017: 4). In this book, we have been raising critical questions about what kinds of orientations and artefacts we are turning towards or away from in regard to media engagement – and within what social environments. It is our contention that

DOI: 10.4324/9781003179481-11

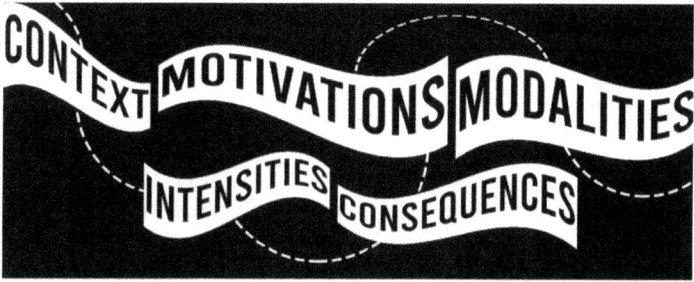

Figure 8.1 'Parameters of media engagement' graphic illustration by J.C. Lee

the present historical juncture in many societies is marked by dramatic processes that are engendering an array of short- and longer-term transformations: we are witnessing not only a global pandemic, but still more significantly an acute rise in populism within older and newer democracies, and a deepening of autocratic measures in non-democratic ones. Power, and the relations around it, are at stake, as is, by extension, freedom.

Our case study examples range from shorter illustrations of commercialised entertainment and audience engagement, to in-depth research on news and public information in Malaysia and Vietnam, and the Belarusian protests during the period of 2020–2021. These two in-depth cases illustrate different democratic and authoritarian systems, including structural failures during the global pandemic regarding public information, or citizen access to political and economic resources during the crisis. As situated case studies, the research offers local examples of engagement, including heterogeneous modes of engagement. At the same time, the cases also offer global examples of engagement, including homogeneous modes of engagement during the pandemic crisis and post-pandemic society. Thus, through the case study research, we illustrate patterns and variations of political and media engagement with different degrees of control of information flows, knowledge and trust, citizen commitment, or precarity of income. Our hope is that they serve as pedagogic illustrations of the centrality and dynamics of media (dis)engagement. We leave it to you, our readers, to apply the perspectives we present to circumstances closer to your own.

CASE STUDIES

To return to the opening example of smartphone friendship, a glimpse into the fiercely competitive environment of entertainment platforms and mobile phone applications illuminated the affective bonds formed through engagement with a technical device. The way an audience member, a young Chinese-Malay, reflected on their modes of engagement with a smartphone alerted us to the meaning of engagement as relational. We can see cognitive, affective and emotional relations, for example, a phone as friend, dinner companion, information provider and commercial entertainment dealer; and we can see local and global relations, for example, Netflix as an international distributor of content and how the platform giant has muscled in on local cable and television provision in Southeast Asia. These dynamics of engagement suggest contradictory power relations (Freedman 2014), simultaneously opening up consumer engagement with a range of uncensored and global drama, documentary, or reality TV, and locking consumers into contracts, devices and digital infrastructures that are needed to generate a 'Netflix entertainment park', a digital space that encroaches on national channels, public service media and local content (Hill and Lee 2021).

For the example of populism and professional wrestling in Chapter 2, in live sports entertainment, the performance of wrestlers and the crafting of a narrative based on the rise of populism in Europe and the Brexit referendum allowed us to see intensities of engagement by audiences and fans. In a live event, wrestlers shape the subjective realities of the crowd through their invitation to engage with a live match. The spectrum of engagement is part of the multi-dimensional experience of a live crowd, including highly physical engagement that is intrinsic to the affective structures and mood for a live event (see Chow, Laine and Warden 2016; Laine, 2019; Hill 2018). In this case, a spectrum of engagement includes both positive emotional engagement with a wrestler performing a hero (the migrant worker), and negative engagement with a villain (the right wing politician). We can see how affective relations are key to the way the parameters of engagement connect together, from the context of political cultures and populism in Europe, to the modes of positive and negative engagement that drive the story, as the crowd cheers and boos in time with the wrestlers who need the attention of the crowd – disengagement is to be avoided at all costs, effectively creating a negative experience and discouraging repeat business. We analysed the case as an example of the intersections of engaging with political and popular culture, signalling how symbolic and economic power can be understood through the affective relations between performers and their live audiences and fans, within the commercial world of professional wrestling.

We began the introductory chapter to the book with an example of smartphone friendship, in particular the communication infrastructures for aggressively commercial streaming platforms targeting mobile social media publics in Southeast Asia, thus providing a snapshot of the intrinsic affective relations of media engagement. In Chapter 2, we illustrated the five parameters of media engagement with an example of populism in professional wrestling, thus providing an in-depth analysis of the connections across popular entertainment, and live events and experiences, and political cultures in the Nordic region. In Chapters 5, 6 and 7, we turned our attention to the case of varying degrees of (dis)trust in news in Malaysia and Vietnam, and protests in Belarus against a crackdown on communicative rights and citizen action, illustrations of media and political engagement within COVID-19 cultures of citizenship and social protest. Our in-depth case studies, conducted during 2021-2022, hit home how the multi-form crises of COVID-19 (e.g. health, education and employment) and the politics of the pandemic (e.g. government policies and elections) provide a spot light, perhaps even a search light, on 'the insurgency of unheard' citizens within society and culture (Coleman 2017: 118, see also Sunstein 2017).

In Belarus, the pandemic was met by outright denial from the autocratic regime. This attempt at reality definition by proclamation not only proved to be futile, it also ironically served as a catalyst for engendering civic cultures: knowledge was shared horizontally in society by health workers to counter the information blackout by the regime; new bonds of trust emerged as citizens began to share information and establish solidarity: an unprecedented civic trust began to take shape in a society that previously had weak civic bonds. Anger and indignation underscored humanitarian and democratic values; crucially, citizens began making more use of available online communication spaces, as well as occupying physical spaces for interaction. Engagement was galvanising, and in the process, citizens began developing an array of practices to spread information about the pandemic. New civic identities were taking shape, though at first quite inchoate. By the time that the true results of the election were denied and Lukashenko, the sitting president, declared the winner, a proto-civic culture of resistance was already in place. It was robust and energising, and manifested itself publicly in massive ways that obviously threatened the regime. The protests were brutally crushed, and new, ever more draconian measures were enacted. Yet the memory of this civic culture, and the brief experience of democratic agency it offered, remains – with many citizens waiting for new opportunities for the democratic reconstruction of their society, where their voices can be heard.

In Southeast Asia, the interviews with news audiences record their voices as ongoing struggles to find a voice (see also Couldry 2010). The emphasis on the negation of news, and processes of (dis)engagement and (dis)trust in official news from Malaysia and Vietnam, is a study of silence and discontent – of struggle and resilience. For the interviews conducted with Vietnamese millennials during the COVID-19 crisis, this is one voice talking about the 'Vietnamese situation': 'I know about it, people know about it but don't talk about it' (30-year-old male graphic designer). When listening to this voice, the interviewer observed 'I see myself and I feel myself in every single word he says'.[1] In this absence of meaningful spaces for democratic debate, struggles to find a voice become spaces of resilience. Here, then, the meaning of engagement can be connected to resonance, which takes into account sociopolitical contexts. Resonance means 'an intrinsic connection or correspondence of mutual relation' (Rosa 2019: 58). Resonance also means 'what ripples and radiates: one energetic being influences the vibrations of another' (Bogart 2021: 3). Our meaning of engagement as a nexus of relations intertwines with this meaning of resonance. One person's voice about their (dis)engagement with the Communist Party–controlled news and information resonates with another person listening to them.

Media engagement consists of mutual relations that influence ourselves and others. We identify five of these relations in our parameters model: context, motivations, modalities, intensities and consequences of engagement. These five parts relate to each other. For example, the context to Malaysian and Vietnamese news, such as strictures on media freedom that serve to enforce state power and promote the political agenda of the governing party, relates to motivations to not engage with official news by millennials in our study. Although we isolate each parameter to identify the salient data and analysis, each parameter works with the others, to create a tone of engagement overall. The person interviewed above who talked about knowing and yet not knowing too much about politics, except with trusted friends and family, and even then with some caution, knows how and why they disengage with news. In this example, their news and political (dis)engagement resonates with despair; a feeling that democratic spaces, in social media, broadcast news, or in public spheres are far beyond their reach.

Earlier in the book, in Chapters 1 and 2, we referred to a music metaphor of chordal relations, for example, a tonal arrangement for media engagement. We have in mind the way affect and rhythm work together across our subjective and bodily encounters with media (Blackman 2012). For Henriques et al (2014: 4), there are conceptual resonances with 'rhythm and such notions as affect, virtuality and power'; they are referring to earlier work on rhythm-analysis by French theorist Henri Lefebvre (1996/2003) and recent cultural and philosophical analysis on a return to rhythm in research on affect. For our purposes, the suggestion of rhythm as 'an affective charge, conveying meaning as feeling and tone, rather than logic of information' (Henriques et al 2014: 4) is useful in considering the more affective relations in media engagement, such as intensities of engagement and a meaning of affect as vibrations we feel in different ways.

Throughout the book, and never more so than in this conclusion, we noted how context is key to the parameters of engagement. We can say that context is much like the chosen key of a song, along with its basic note intervals and harmonies. Beyond that we have melody, rhythm, perhaps more advanced harmonies, as well as dynamics, phrasing and so on – that is, our other parameters. Without knowing the key and basic harmonies, one cannot begin to sing or play along with others, but with that in place, one can then turn one's attention to the melody and other elements and join in. All the musical elements, working together, collectively lift and define a particular tonal mood. Thus, a tonal mood of engagement is compounded by affective relations, but it is also part of flows of information and public knowledge in the context of media systems, sociopolitical infrastructures and histories.

For example, in the case of news engagement in Vietnam, the news media has a historical context of ideological projects carried out by the Communist Party to educate populations, such as women being targeted regarding the ideal of the happy and harmonious family life (Horton and Rydstrom 2019). News via the internet and social media offers an alternative source of information, in particular citizen bloggers and journalists producing for digital platforms, but this is tempered by the concomitant rise of online Vietnamese nationalism. News engagement in one setting of national media resonates in another setting of digital journalism.

In such a way, we can start to understand the tone of news engagement as part of a pervasive culture of negation in this region, a major finding of our analysis of this case (see Chapters 5 and 6). The media, political and societal contexts for news engagement are an affective arrangement as it were. And this arrangement for news engagement starts out in a certain key, and then the other parts of the parameters, such as motivations, or modalities, form the chordal relations. For someone growing up with news in Vietnam, during a similar time period and familial environment, this sounds familiar – hence the way one voice from an interview has such emotional resonance for the interviewer and their own news media and political experiences. We can isolate the individual parameters (as chords) – for example, modalities of online news through the platform of Twitter or TikTok, but we also want to listen to the parameters together (as an arrangement of chords), which are set within a certain context (the key for this arrangement).

In Belarus, the state-controlled traditional mass media aimed to define a delimited reality that served the interests of the regime. It made uninspiring, dour music, especially as the younger generation was gaining access to the wider world through digital media. By the time the protests broke out, the digital platform Telegram became the collective voice of the oppositional movement, with arousing melodies, inspiring harmonies and intense rhythms. When the protests were crushed and media control further extended, the silence was loud.

If we want to understand the contingencies and contradictions of media engagement, then isolating each of the parameters enables us to identify how, when and in what way engagement is a marker of power relations. We hope this sense of media engagement allows us to think through engagement as part of a broader context, for example, historical, societal, technological, or cultural, that offers us perspectives on audiences and citizens and their 'psychological orientations to the world and to the artefacts within it' (Corner 2017: 4).

REFLECTIONS

When we started our research on the parameters of media engagement, it was a period of time where populism was on the rise, for example, in the form of the British referendum on exiting the European Union, which resulted in Brexit. At the time of writing the short, sharply analytical book *Can the Internet Strengthen Democracy?*, Stephen Coleman (2017) noted in post-Brexit Britain a list of concerns – distorted information, impoverished public debate and the infantilisation of voting citizens. These concerns suggested to Coleman 'the spaces for meaningful and consequential public exchange of ideas and experiences are in worrying short supply' (2017: vi). This was a book written for readers who may 'share these worries and are prepared to take a stand for something better' (2017: viii).

Pertinent to our work on engagement, Coleman identified that in such a divisive political climate 'citizens must be capable of knowing and showing who they are but they must also know where they are and what is going on around them' (2017: 89). Engagement with various forms of media distributed through mainstream and alternative platforms can offer pathways for citizens towards democracy: 'mutual recognition and respect is not a mere precursor to democratic politics, but is the very essence of politics, which entails an ongoing struggle to be counted as one who matters' (2017: 110). We have seen that this desire to be seen, to be heard, to have voice, is very much at the fore among the citizens in our presentations from Malaysia and Vietnam, and Belarus, but it has also become a major concern in democratic societies; indeed perceptions of its absence are having a critical and even destabilising impact on democracy.

Our book starts with an idea of media engagement as a nexus of relations that can tell us something about power. And our short book is written during the global pandemic and COVID times, a health crisis that has alerted us to the critical study of crisis as connected to media engagement and resistance, even, at times, resilience. The identification of COVID-19 in Wuhan, China, in 2020, and its ensuing catastrophic impact on global infrastructures, societies, cultures and citizens, is a crisis that breaks down infrastructures and breaks apart families, communities and societies, including movement restriction orders, isolation and human precarity. At the same time, it is a crisis that also affords political and sociocultural contestation and renewal through, and hopefully beyond, the health pandemic (Walby 2015; Crouch 2020). The 'insurgency of the unheard' that Coleman (2017: 118) noted during the aftermath of Brexit in the UK is even more significant at the time of writing our book and COVID-19 cultures of citizenship.

The examples of the Belarus protests, and negation of news in Southeast Asia, are a part of social contingencies of media and political engagement, and the precarity of the present-day COVID-19 crisis, with all that this entails for getting by under challenging conditions. In Belarus, the state-controlled media was the background minor-key symbolic environment to daily life. The new but short-lived oppositional digital media provided an exuberant alternative, a promise of a new way of life. Globally, audiences and citizens are already attuned to their media engagement as relational; they identify the parts that connect with their whole lives. As researchers, we can try to tune in to those who struggle to find a voice. As citizens, we must all ensure that we have a sustained voice, in whatever sets of power relations we find ourselves in.

NOTE

1   Interviewer Ha Linh Trang Nguyen in email correspondence with authors 17 December 2021.

APPENDIX

NEWS ENGAGEMENT INTERVIEW GUIDE

NEWS CONTEXT

Where do you go for specific types of information/content?

> *Medium: Print/Broadcast/Computer/Mobile devices*
> *Sources: Publications/Broadcasters/Websites/Groups*
> *Online platforms: Messaging applications/Social networking sites*

How (and when) did you learn to look for information/content through these means?

What is your opinion of the sources and platforms where you get this information/content?

> *Politics, ownership, controversy*
> *What is your opinion on how it filters information/content for you?*
> *What are the pros and cons of getting information/content through*
> *these means?*

NEWS MOTIVATIONS

What motivates you to check the news?

> *Personal, social, professional, political*
> *How and when did you learn to keep up with news?*

What makes news relevant to you?

Are there any events in the news that you are anticipating, and what are they?

> *How come?*

NEWS MODALITIES

How would you compare the experience (analysis/focus and emotion) of getting information/content in print, over broadcast or online?

> *Online: Computers/Mobile phones*
> *Genres: Political/Sports/Entertainment*

How do you know when to trust information/content?

> *How did you learn to tell whether such information/content is truthful?*
> *What do you do if something does not appear truthful?*
> *Does it matter when and where you get this information/content?*

What kind of mood must you be in to engage with news?

NEWS INTENSITIES

How much effort do you put into looking for such information/content?

> *Light: Editorial/Algorithmic/Notifications/Shared*
> *Heavy: Search/Compare/Discuss*
> *Place and time*

Do you share or discuss news with any groups?

> *Friends/Family/Communities*
> *How many people are in these groups?*
> *What kinds of news do you share and discuss?*
> *Does it feel different getting news from these groups?*

NEWS CONSEQUENCES (PERSONAL, SOCIAL, POLITICAL)

What is your opinion on national news organisations/journalists?

> *Mainstream/Alternative*
> *National/Regional (Asian/Language)/International*
> *Too many/Too few*
> *Do you get news from sources other than news organisations, and what are they?*

How would you compare your news habits to those of your friends and family?

> *Do you share, discuss news with them often?*
> *How much do you depend on them for news?*
> *How careful are they with information? (Accurate, comprehensive)*
> *What would you do when they are not careful with information? (Responsibility)*

What do you do with all this news? (Personal, social, political)

> *To socialise*
> *To be entertained*
> *To fulfil political/civic responsibilities*

What happens when you don't keep up with news?

OTHER

Is there anything else you'd like to add?

References

Ahtola, Dan. (2018) Interview with Annette Hill (27 September), audio recording. Lund, Sweden.

Alexander, Jeffery, Elisabeth Bultler Breese and María Luengo, eds. (2016) *The Crisis of Journalism Reconsidered: Democratic Culture, Professional Codes, Digital Future.* New York: Cambridge University Press.

Allan, Stuart. (2004) *News Culture.* 2nd ed. Berkshire: McGraw-Hill Education.

Amnesty International. (2016) Critical crackdown: freedom of expression under attack in Malaysia. Available online: www.amnesty.org/download/Docume nts/ASA2831662016ENGLISH.PDF

Anderson, Ben. (2014) *Encountering Affect: Capacities, Apparatuses, Conditions.* Farnham: Ashgate.

Anderson, Monica, Skye Toor, Lee Rainie and Aaron Smith. (2018) *Activism in the Social Media Age.* Pew Research Center. Available online: www.pewinter net.org/2018/07/11/public-attitudes-toward-political-engagement-on-soc ial-media/

Andrejevic, Mark. (2013) *Infoglut: How Too Much Information Is Changing the Way We Think and Know.* Abingdon: Routledge.

Arendt, Hannah. (1958) *The Human Condition.* Chicago, IL: University of Chicago Press.

Arvidsson, Adam and Tizanio Bonini. (2015) 'Valuing audience passions: From Smythe to Tarde'. *European Journal of Cultural Studies* 18 (2): 158–173.

Asen, Robert and Daniel C. Brouwer, eds. (2001) *Counterpublics and the State.* Albany, NY: State University of New York Press.

Asmolov, Gregory. (2020) 'The path to the square: the role digital technologies in Belarus protests'. *Open Democracy.* Available online: www.opendemocracy. net/en/odr/path-to-square-digital-technology-belarus-protest/

Bakardjieva, Maria, Stina Bengtsson, Göran Bolin and Kjell Engelbrekt. (2021) *Digital Media and the Dynamics of Civil Society: Retooling Citizenship in New EU Democracies.* Lanham, MD: Rowman & Littlefield.

Bartlett, Jamie. (2018) *The People vs. Tech.* London: Ebury Press.

Baxandall, Rosalyn and Linda Gordon, eds. (2000) *Dear Sisters: Dispatches from the Women's Liberation Movement.* New York: Basic Books.

Baym, Nancy K. (2015) *Personal Connections in the Digital Age.* 2nd ed. Cambridge: Polity Press.

BBC News. (2020) Vietnam: Facebook and Google 'complicit' in censorship. Available online: www.bbc.com/news/world-asia-55140857

Beck, Ulrich. (1998) *Democracy Without Enemies.* Cambridge: Polity Press.

Bekus, Nelly. (2021) 'Echo of 1989? Protest imaginaries and identity dilemmas in Belarus'. *Slavic Review* 80 (1): 4–14.

Bengtsson, Stina and Sofia Johansson. (2020) 'A phenomenology of news: understanding news in digital culture'. *Journalism*. Epub ahead of print 27 January, 2020. doi:10.1177/1464884919901194

Benkler, Yochai, Robert Faris and Hal Roberts. (2018) *Network Propaganda: Manipulation, Disinformation and Radicalization in American Politics*. Oxford: Oxford University Press.

Bennett, W. Lance. (2003) 'Lifestyle politics and citizen-consumers: identity, communication and political action in late modern society'. In John Corner and Dick Pels, eds. *Media and Political Style: Essays on Representation and Civic Culture*. London: Sage, pp. 137–150.

Bennett, W. Lance and Alexandra Segerberg. (2013) *The Logic of Connective Action: Digital Media and the Personalization of Contentious Politics*. New York: Cambridge University Press.

Bhattacherjee, Anol. (2012) *Social Science Research: Principles, Methods and Practices*. London: Sage.

Blackman, Lisa. (2012) *Immaterial Bodies: Affect, Embodiment, Mediation*. Los Angeles, CA: Sage.

Bogart, Anne. (2021) *The Art of Resonance*. London: Bloomsbury Publishing.

Bolin, Goran. (2017) *Media Generations: Experience, Identity and Mediatised Social Change*. New York, London: Routledge.

Börjel, Ida and Mikael Nydahl. (2021) 'Introduktion'. In Ida Börjel and Mikael Nydahl, eds. *Ett år i Belarus. Röster inifrån en folkresning (One Year in Belarus: Voices from a Popular Uprising)*. Stockholm: Atlas, pp. 1–18.

Brenner, Neil, Jamie Peck and Nick Theodore. (2010) 'Variegated neoliberalization: Geographies, modalities, pathways'. *Global Networks* 10 (2): 182–222.

Bröckling, Ulrich. (2016) *The Entrepreneurial Self: Fabricating a New Type of Subject*. London: Sage.

Brown, Wendy. (2015) *Undoing the Demos: Neoliberalism's Stealth Revolution*. New York: Zone Books.

Brown, Wendy. (2019) *In the Ruins of Neoliberalism: The Rise of Antidemocratic Politics in the West*. New York: Columbia University Press.

Brunsdon, Charlotte and David Morley. (1978) *Everyday Television: Nationwide*. British Film Institute.

Bucher, Tania. (2018) *If... Then: Algorithmic Power and Politics*. Cambridge: Cambridge University Press.

Bui, Thiem Hai. (2016) 'The influence of social media in Vietnam's elite politics'. *Journal of Current Southeast Asian Affairs* 35 (2): 89–111.

Burns, Anna. (2018) *Milkman*. London: Faber and Faber.

Butter, Michael and Peter Knight, eds. (2021) *The Routledge Handbook of Conspiracy Theories*. Abingdon: Routledge.

Butter, Peter. (2020) *The Nature of Conspiracy Theories*. Cambridge: Polity Press. Byford, Jovan. (2011) *Conspiracy Theories: A Critical Introduction*. Houndmills, Basingstoke: Palgrave Macmillan.

Byrne, Janet, ed. (2012) *The Occupy Handbook*. New York: Backbay Books/Little, Brown and Co.

Calhoun, Craig, ed. (1992) *Habermas and the Public Sphere*. Boston, MA: MIT Press.

Cammaerts, Bart and Leo van Audenhove. (2003) *Transnational Social Movements, the Network Society and Unbounded Notions of Citizenship*. Amsterdam: ASCoR, University of Amsterdam.

Canovan, Margaret. (1981) *Populism*. London: Junction.

Carlson, Matt, Sue Robinson and Seth C. Lewis. (2021) *News After Trump: Journalism's Crisis of Relevance*. New York: Oxford University Press.

Carpentier, Nico. (2011) *Media and Participation: A Site of Ideological-Democratic Struggle*. Bristol: Intellect.

Carr, Nicholas. (2014) *The Glass Cage: How Our Computers Are Changing Us*. New York: Norton.

Cassin, Barbara. (2017) *Google Me: One-Click Democracy*. New York: Fordham University Press.

Castells, Manuel. (2012) *Networks of Outrage and Hope: Social Movements in the Internet Age*. Cambridge: Polity Press.

Castleberry, Garret, Carrielynn Reinhard, Matt Foy and Christopher Olson. (2018) 'Introduction: Why professional wrestling studies now?' *The Popular Culture Studies Journal* 6 (1): 65–80.

Centre for Independent Journalism. (2020) The future of media freedom in Malaysia, a World Press Freedom Day 2020 message, 3 May. Available online: https://cijmalaysia.net/the-future-of-media-freedom-in-malaysia-a-world-press-freedom-day-2020-message/

Cheah, Charissa S.L., Christy Y.Y. Leung and Sevgi Bayram Özdemir. (2018) 'Chinese Malaysian adolescents' social-cognitive reasoning regarding filial piety dilemmas'. *Child Development* 89 (2): 383–396.

Chinnasamy, Sara. (2018) *New Media Political Engagement and Participation in Malaysia*. Abingdon: Routledge.

Chow, Broderick, Eero Laine and Claire Warden. (2016) *Performance and Professional Wrestling*. London: Sage.

Chowdovnik, Magdalena and Omar Marques. (2021) 'The essence of Belarusian solidarity'. *New Eastern Europe* XLVIII 5: 30–41.

Clapp, Rodney. (2021) *Naming Neoliberalism: Expressing the Spirit of Our Age*. Minneapolis, MN: Fortress Press.

Cobble, Dorothy Sue, Linda Gordon and Astrid Henry. (2014) *Feminism Unfinished: A Short, Surprising History of American Women's Movements*. New York: Liveright Publishing/Norton.

Coleman, Stephen. (2013) *How Voters Feel*. Cambridge: Cambridge University Press.

Coleman, Stephen. (2017) *Can the Internet Strengthen Democracy?* Cambridge: Polity Press.

Coleman, Stephen and Jim Brogden. (2020) *Capturing the Mood of Democracy: The British General Election 2019*. Cham: Palgrave-Macmillan/Springer.

Collins, Patricia Hill. (2019) *Intersectionality as Critical Social Theory*. Durham, NC: Duke University Press.

Colvile, Robert. (2016) *The Great Acceleration*. London: Bloomsbury.

Corner, John. (2011) *Theorising Media*. Manchester: Manchester University Press.

Corner, John. (2017) 'Afterword'. *Media Industries* (4) (1): 1–6.

Couldry, Nick. (2010) *Why Voice Matters: Culture and Politics After Neoliberalism*. London: Sage.

Couldry, Nick. (2014) 'The myth of "us": digital networks, political change and the production of collectivity'. *Information, Communication & Society*. 18 (6): 608–626, doi:10.1080/1369118X.2014.979216

Couldry, Nick, Sonia Livingstone and Tim Markham. (2007) *Media Consumption and Public Engagement: Beyond the Presumption of Attention*. Basingstoke: Intellect.

Couldry, Nick and Ulises A. Mejias. (2019) *The Costs of Connection: How Data Is Colonizing Human Life and Appropriating It for Capitalism*. Stanford, CA: Stanford University Press.

Crouch, Colin. (2020) *Post-Democracy: After the Crises*. Cambridge: Polity Press.

Croucher, Stephen A. and Daniel Cronn-Mills. (2022) *Understanding Communication Research Methods: A Theoretical and Practical Approach*. 3rd ed. New York: Routledge.

Crozier, Michel, Samuel Huntington and Joji Watanuki. (1975) *The Crisis of Democracy: Report on the Governability of Democracies to the Trilateral Commission*. New York: New York University Press.

Cushion, Stephen, Declan McDowell-Naylor and Richard Thomas. (2021) 'Why national media systems matter: a longitudinal analysis of how UK left-wing and right-wing alternative media critique mainstream media (2015–2018). *Journalism Studies* 22 (5): 633–652.

Dahlgren, Peter. (2009) *Media and Political Engagement: Citizens, Communication, and Democracy*. New York: Cambridge University Press.

Dahlgren, Peter. (2013) *The Political Web: Participation, Media, and Alternative Democracy*. Basingstoke: Palgrave Macmillan.

Dahlgren, Peter and Annette Hill. (2020) 'Parameters of media engagement'. *Media Theory* 4 (19): 1–32.

Dawes, Simon and Marc Lenormand, eds. (2020) *Neoliberalism in Context: Governance, Subjectivity and Knowledge*. London: Palgrave Macmillan.

DeBenedetti, Charles. (1990) *An American Ordeal: The Antiwar Movement in the Vietnam Era*. Syracuse: Syracuse University Press.

della Porta, Donatello and Mario Diani, eds. (2016) *The Oxford Handbook of Social Movements*. Oxford: Oxford University Press.

della Porta, Donatello and Mario Diani. (2020) *Social Movements: An Introduction*. Oxford: Wiley Blackwell.

Department of Statistics Malaysia. (2020) Current population estimates, Malaysia, 2020. Available online: www.dosm.gov.my/v1/index.php?r=column/cthemeByCat&cat=155&bul_id=OVByWjg5YkQ3MWFZRTN5bDJiaEVhZz09&menu_id=LopheU43NWJwRWVSZklWdzQ4TlhUUT09

Deutsche Welle. (2021) Vietnam jails pro-democracy journalists for 'propaganda'. Available online: www.dw.com/en/vietnam-jails-3-journalists-for-state-critical-propaganda/a-56132070

Dierenfield, Bruce J. (2021) *The Civil Rights Movement*. New York: Routledge.

Dimock, Michael. (2019) Defining generations: where millennials end and Generation Z begins. Available online: www.pewresearch.org/fact-tank/2019/01/17/where-millennials-end-and-generation-z-begins/

Doona, Joanna. (2018) 'Political comedy engagement: identity and community construction'. *European Journal of Cultural Studies* 23 (4): 531–547.

Downing, John D.H. (2001) *Radical Media: Rebellious Communication and Social Movements*. London: Sage.

Duong, Mai. (2017) 'Blogging three ways in Vietnam's political blogosphere'. Available online: https://muse.jhu.edu/article/667781. *Contemporary Southeast Asia* 39 (2): 373–392.

Eatwell, Roger and Matthew Goodwin. (2018) *National Populism: The Revolt Against Liberal Democracy*. London: Pelican.

Edgerly, Stephanie and Emily Vraga. (2020) 'Deciding what's news: News-ness as an audience concept for the hybrid media environment'. *Journalism & Mass Communication Quarterly* 97 (2): 416–434.

Edgerton, David. (2007) *The Shock of the Old: Technology and Global History Since 1900*. Oxford: Oxford University Press.

Eliasoph, Nina. (1997) 'Close to home: the work of avoiding politics'. *Theory and Society* 26: 605–647.

Eliasoph, Nina. (1998) *Avoiding Politics: How Americans Produce Apathy in Everyday Life*. Cambridge: Cambridge University Press.

Elliott, Anthony. (2019) *The Culture of AI*. London: Routledge.

Eriksson, Stefan. (2021) 'Belarus. En nations återfödelse' (Belarus: a nations's rebirth). In Ida Börjel and Mikael Nydahl, eds. *Ett år I Belarus. Röster inifrån en folkresning (One Year in Belarus: Voices From Within a Popular Uprising)*. Stockholm: Atlas, pp. 111–132.

Evans, Elizabeth. (2019) *Understanding Engagement in Transmedia Cultures*. London: Routledge.

Faderman, Lillian. (2015) *The Gay Revolution: The Story of the Struggle*. New York: Simon and Schuaster.

Farkas, Johan and Jannick Schou. (2020) *Post-Truth, Fake News and Democracy*. Abingdon: Routledge.

Fassin, Didier and Bernard Harcourt, eds. (2019) *A Time for Critique*. New York: Columbia University Press.

Felski, Rita. (2015) *The Limits of Critique*. Chicago, IL: University of Chicago Press.

Ferrer-Conill, Raul and Edson C. Tandoc Jr. (2018) 'The audience-oriented editor'. *Digital Journalism* 6 (4): 436–453.

Filipenko, Sasja. (2021) 'Kröniker och öppna brev' (chronicles and open letters). In Ida Börjel and Mikael Nydahl, eds. *Ett år i Belarus: Röster inifrån en folkresning (One Year in Belarus: Voices from within a People's Uprising)*. Stockholm: Atlas, pp. 111–132.

Franklin, Bob, ed. (2016) *The Future of News: In an Age of Digital Media and Economic Uncertainty*. Abingdon: Routledge.

Fraser, Nancy. (1992) 'Rethinking the public sphere: a contribution to the crtitique of actually existing democracy'. In Craig Calhoun, ed. *Habermas and the Public Sphere*. Boston, MA: MIT Press, pp. 109–142.

Freedman, Des. (2014) *The Contradictions of Media Power*. London: Bloomsbury Press.

Friedland, Lewis A., Thomas Hove and Hernando Rojas. (2006) 'The networked public sphere'. *Javnost/The Public* 13 (4): 5–26.

Frosh, Stephen. (2011) *Feelings*. Abingdon: Routledge.

Fuchs, Christian. (2021) *Social Media: A Critical Introduction*. 3rd ed. London: Sage.

Fung, Cheryl W. L. (2020) 'Canvas of dissent: a study of visuals and their significance in group formations and communications during the 2019 Hong Kong anti-ELAB movement'. In Joanna Doona, ed. *Excellent Msc. Dissertations*. Lund: Lund University. pp. 61–110.

Gabowitsch, Mischa. (2021) 'Belarusian protest: regimes of engagement and coordination'. *Slavic Review* 80 (1): 27–37.

Gallup. (2015) The changing media landscape in Vietnam. Available online: www.bbg.gov/wp-content/media/2015/06/Vietnam-Event-Final.pdf

Gapova, Elena. (2021) 'Class, agency and citizenship in Belarusian protest'. *Slavic Review* 80 (1): 45–51.

Gauntlett, David and Annette Hill. (1997) *TV Living*. London: Routledge.

George, Cherian. (2005) The internet's political impact and the penetration/participation paradox in Malaysia and Singapore. *Media, Culture & Society* 27 (6): 903–920. doi:10.1177/0163443705057678

George, Cherian. (2007) 'Media in Malaysia: zone of contention'. *Democratization* 14 (5): 893–910. doi:10.1080/13510340701635712

Gerdžiūnas, Benas. (2020, 20 September) Revolution will be telegrammed; social media channels drive Belarus protests'. *Euraktiv*. Available online: www.euractiv.com/section/digital/news/revolution-will-be-telegrammed-social-media-channels-drive-belarus-protest

Gilroy-Ware, Marcus. (2017) *Filling the Void: Emotion, Capitalism and Social Media*. London: Repeater Books.

Gitlin, Todd. (2003/1980) *The Whole World is Watching*. Berkeley: University of California Press.

Gitlin, Todd. (2012) *Occupy Nation*. New York: HaperCollins/IT Books.

Gray, Anne. (1982) *Video Playtime: The Gendering of a Leisure Technology*. London: Routledge.

Gray, Jonathan. (2021) *Dislike Minded*. New York: New York University Press.

Gregg, Melissa and Gregory J. Seigworth, eds. (2010) *The Affect Theory Reader*. Durham, NC: Duke University Press.

Gubrium, Jaber and James Holstein. (2014) Analytic inspiration in ethnographic fieldwork. In Uwe Flick, ed. *The SAGE Handbook of Qualitative Data Analysis*. London: Sage, pp. 35–48.

Habermas, Jürgen. (1989) *Structural Transformation of the Public Sphere*. Cambridge: Polity Press.

Habermas, Jürgen. (1996) *Between Facts and Norms*. Cambridge, MA: MIT Press.

Habermas, Jürgen. (2006) 'Political communication in mediated society'. *Communication Research* 16 (4): 411–426.

Haglund, Dina. (2021) ' "Det är vår uppgift att skydda och bevara Belarus kulurella identitet" '. (It is our task to protect and preserve Belarusian cultural identity). *Dagen nyheter*, 14 February, p. 5.

Hall, Cheryl. (2005) *The Trouble with Passion: Political Theory Beyond the Reign of Reason*. New York: Routledge.

Harte, David, Rachel Howells and Andy Williams. (2018) *Hyperlocal Journalism: The Decline of Local Newspapers and the Rise of Online Community News*. London: Routledge.

Harvey, David. (2007) *A Brief History of Neoliberalism*. New York: Oxford University Press.

Hay, Colin. (2007) *Why We Hate Politics*. Cambridge: Polity Press.

Hayton, Bill. (2010) *Vietnam: Rising Dragon*. New Haven, CT: Yale University Press.

Head, Jonathan. (2020) *How Malaysia's government collapsed in two years* [Online]. Available at: www.bbc.com/news/world-asia-51716474

Held, David. (2006) *Models of Democracy*. 3rd ed. Cambridge: Polity Press.

Heng, Russell Hiang-Khng. (2002) *Media Fortunes, changing times: ASEAN States in Transition*. Singapore: Institute of Southeast Asian Studies.

Henriques, Julian, Milla Tiainen and Pasi Valiaho. (2014) 'Rhythm returns: movement and cultural theory'. *Body & Society* 20 (3&4): 3–29.

Hermes, Joke. (1984) *Reading Women's Magazines: An Analysis of Everyday Media Use*. London: Wiley.

Hermes, Joke. (2005) *Re-reading Popular Culture*. Oxford: Blackwell.

Hermes, Joke. (2012) The scary promise of technology: developing new forms of audience research. In G. Bolin, ed. *Cultural Technologies: The Shaping of Culture in Media and Society*. New York: Routledge, pp. 189–201.

Highfield, Tim. (2016) *Social Media and Everyday Politics*. Cambridge: Polity Press.

Hiley, David R. (2006) *Doubt and the Demands of Democratic Citizenship*. Cambridge: Cambridge University Press.

Hill, Annette. (2007) *Restyling Factual TV*. London: Routledge.

Hill, Annette. (2015) *Reality TV*. London: Routledge.

Hill, Annette. (2017) 'Reality TV engagement: producers and audiences for talent format *Got to Dance*'. *Media Industries* 4 (1): 1–17.

Hill, Annette. (2018) *Media Experiences: Engaging with Drama and Reality Entertainment*. London: Routledge.

Hill, Annette and Jeanette Steemers. (2017) 'Introduction to media engagement'. *Media Industries* 4 (1): 1–5.

Hill, Annette and Jian Chung Lee. (2021) 'Roamers: audiences in the move across entertainment platforms in Southeast Asia'. *Javnost – The Public*, online first.

Hill, Annette, Jian Chung Lee and Ha Linh Trang Nguyen. (forthcoming) 'News engagement and social resilience in Southeast Asia'.

Hill, Annette, Tina Askanius, Koko Kondo and Jose Luis Urueta. (2019) 'Provocative engagement: documentary audiences and performances in *The Act of*

Killing and *The Look of Silence'*. *International Journal of Cultural Studies* 22 (5): 662–677.

Holt, Thomas C. (2021) *The Movement: The African American Struggle for Civil Rights.* New York: Oxford University Press.

Horton, Paul and Helle Rydstrom. (2019) 'Reshaping boundaries: family politics and GLBTQ resistance in urban Vietnam'. *Journal of GLBT Family Studies* 15 (3): 290–305.

Human Rights Watch. (2019) Malaysia: end use of Sedition Act, 17 July. Available online: www.hrw.org/news/2019/07/17/malaysia-end-use-sedition-act

Hutton, Clare. (2019) 'The moment and technique of milkman'. *Essays in Criticism* 69 (3): 349–369.

Jackson, Maggie. (2009) *Distracted: The Erosion of Attention and the Coming Dark Age.* New York: Prometheus Books.

Jenkins, Henry, Joshua Green and Sam Ford. (2013) *Spreadable Media: Creating Value and Meaning in a Networked Culture.* New York: New York Press.

Johnson, Sarah. (2021) 'Belarus regime steps up "purge" of activists and media'. *The Guardian* 9 August. Available online: www.theguardian.com/global-developm ent/2021/aug/09/belarus-regime-steps-up-purge-of-activists-and-media

Juris, Jeffrey. (2012) 'Reflections on #Occupy Everywhere: social media, public space, and the emerging logics of aggregation'. *American Ethnologist* 39 (2): 259–279.

Kackman, Michael and Mary Celeste Kearney, eds. (2018) *The Craft of Criticism: Critical Media Studies in Practice.* New York: Routledge.

Kalyango, Yusuf Jr., Folker Hanusch, Jyotika Ramaprasad, Terje Skjerdal, Mohd Safar Hasim, Nurhaya Muchtar, Mohammad Sahid Ullah, Levi Zeleza Manda and Sarah Bomkapre Kamara. (2017) 'Journalists' development journalism role perceptions'. *Journalism Studies* 18 (5): 576–594.

Keightley, Emily and Michael Pickering. (2012) *The Mnemonic Imagination: Remembering as Cultural Practice.* London: Palgrave.

Kendi, Ibram X. (2017) *Stamped from the Beginning: The Definitive History of Racist Ideas in America.* London: Bodley Head/Penguin Random House.Kenyon, Andrew. (2010) 'Investigating chilling effects: news media and public speech in Malaysia, Singapore, and Australia'. *International Journal of Communication* 4: 440–467. Available online: https://search-ebscohost-com.ludwig.lub. lu.se/login.aspx?direct=true&db=edswss&AN=000295486400029&site= eds-live&scope=site

Keucheyan, Razmig. (2013) *The Left Hemisphere: Mapping Critical Theory Today.* London: Verso.

King, Victor T., Phuong An Nguyen and och Nguyen Huu Minh. (2008) 'Professional middle class youth in post-reform Vietnam: identity, continuity and change'. *Modern Asian Studies* 42 (4): 783–813.

Krawatzek, Felix and Gwendolyn Sasse. (2021 4 Feb.) 'Belarus: why people have taken to the streets – new data'. *The Conversation.* Available online: https://thec onversation.com/belarus-protests-why-people-have-been-taking-to-the-stre ets-new-data-154494

Kvale, Steinar. (2007) *Doing Interviews.* London: Sage.

Laine, Eero. (2019) *Professional Wrestling and the Commercial Stage*. London: Routledge.

Laputsla, Veranika. (2021) 'The power of internet as a game changer for Belarusian protests'. *New Eastern Europe* XLVIII 5: 42–47.

Le, Long. (2014) 'With its 'Tiger' status at risk, Vietnam confronts the rise of citizen journalism'. *Global Asia* 9 (2, Summer): 48–53.

Le, Viet T. (2018) 'Two stories: the emergence of the Vietnamese social media'. *Media International Australia* 168 (1): 93–107.Lee, Ester. (2019) The state of the nation: more Malaysians less satisfied with their standard of living, The Edge Markets, 30 December. Available online: www.theedgemarkets.com/arti cle/state-nation-more-malaysians-less-satisfied-their-standard-living

Lee, Jian Chung. (2021) 'Parameters and performances of news engagement: a case study of Swedish audiences'. In J. Doona, ed. *Excellent MSc Dissertations 2020 Media and Communication Studies, Lund University*. Lund: Lund University, pp. 111–154.

Lee, Jian Chung and Ha Linh Trang Nguyen. (2021) Interview for research project, by A Hill.

Lee, Liz and Ungku, Fathin. (2018) Veteran Malaysian leader Mahathir scores shock election win. *Reuters*, 9 May. Available online: www.reuters.com/article/us-malaysia-election-idUSKBN1I93EV

Lefebvre, Henri. (1996/2003) *Writing on Cities*. In E. Kofman and E. Lebas, trans. and ed. Oxford: Blackwell.

Lewis, Simon. (2021) '"Tear down the walls": verses of defiance in the Belarusian revolution. *Slavic Review* 80 (1): 15–26.

Linh Dan. (2021) Vietnam pressures social media platforms to censor. Available online: www.voanews.com/press-freedom/vietnam-pressures-social-media-platforms-censor

Livingstone, Sonia. (2005) 'In defence of privacy: mediating the public/private boundary a home'. In S. Livingstone, ed. *Audiences and Publics: When Cultural Engagement Matters for the Public Sphere*. Bristol: Intellect, pp. 163–185.

Lobato, Ramon and Julian Thomas. (2015) *The Informal Media Economy*. Cambridge: Polity Press.

Loh, Francis and Khoo Boo Teik Khoo. (2002) *Democracy in Malaysia: Discourses and Practises*. London: Routledge.

Lyon, David. (2018) *The Culture of Surveillance: Watching as a Way of Life*. Cambridge: Polity Press.

Mach, Leon and Chris Nash. (2019) 'Social media versus traditional Vietnamese journalism and social power structures'. *Asian Journal of Journalism and Media Studies* 2: 1–14.

Mair, Peter. (2013) *Ruling the Void: The Hollowing of Democracy*. London: Verso.

Malerius, Stephan. (2021) 'One year on: what has changed in Belarus?' *New Eastern Europe* XLVIII (5): 12–20.

Manning, Erin. (2010, April) 'Always more than one: the collectivity of a life'. *Body & Society* 16 (1): 117–127.

Manovich, Lev. (2013) *Software Takes Command*. London: Bloomsbury.

Margetts, Helen, Peter John, Scott Hale and Taha Yasseri. (2016) *Political Turbulence: How Social Media Shape Collective Action*. Princeton, NJ: Princeton University Press.

Marichal, Jose. (2013) 'Political Facebook groups: micro-activism and the digital front stage'. *First Monday* 18 (12). Available online: http://firstmonday.org/ojs/index.php/fm/article/view/4653/3800

Marshall, Thomas Humphrey. (1950) *Citizenship and Social Class*. Cambridge: Cambridge University Press.

Massey, Doreen. (1994) *Space, Place and Gender*. Oxford: Polity Press.

Massumi, Brian. (2002) *Parables for the Virtual: Movement, Affect, Sensation*. Durham, NC: Duke University Press.

McGuigan, Jim. (2016) *Neoliberal Culture*. Basingstoke: Palgrave.

McNair, Brian. (2000) *Journalism and Democracy: An Evaluation of the Political Public Sphere*. London: Routledge.

Meier, Klaus, Daniela Kraus and Edith Michaeler. (2018) 'Audience engagement in a post-truth age'. *Digital Journalism* 6 (8): 1052–1063.

Meijer, Irene Costera and Tim Groot Kormelink. (2014) 'Checking, sharing, clicking and linking'. *Digital Journalism* 3 (5): 664–679.

Meyers, Marian, ed. (2019) *Neoliberalism and the Media*. New York: Routledge.

Micheletti, Michele. (2003) *Political Virtue and Shopping: Individuals, Consumerism, and Collective Action*. New York: Palgrave.

Mill, John Stuart (2002/1859) *On Liberty*. Mineola, NY: Dover Thrift Editions.

Morley, David. (1986) *Family Television: Cultural Power and Domestic Leisure*. Comedia.

Morley, David. (2017) *Communications and Mobility: The Migrant, the Mobile Phone, and the Container Box*. Oxford: Wiley Blackwell.

Morley, David. (2021) 'Mobile socialities: communities, mobilities and boundaries'. In Annette Hill, Maren Hartmann and Magnus Andersson, eds. *The Handbook of Mobile Socialities*. New York: Routledge, pp. 22–37.

Morozov, Evgeny. (2011) *The Net Delusion: How Not to Liberate the World*. London: Allen Lane.

Mouffe, Chantal. (2005) *On the Political*. London: Verso.

Mouffe, Chantal. (2013) *Agonistics: Thinking the World Politically*. London: Verso.

Mudde, Cas and Cristóbal Rovira Kaltwasser. (2017) *Populism: A Very Short Introduction*. New York: Oxford University Press.

Müller, Jan-Werner. (2016) *What is Populism?* Philadelphia, PA: University of Pennsylvania Press.

Nain, Zaharom. (2020) *Reuters Institute Digital News Report 2020*. Available online: www.digitalnewsreport.org/survey/2020/malaysia-2020/

Napoli, Phillip. (2010) *Audience Evolution: New Technologies and the Transformation of Media Audiences*. New York: Columbia University Press.

Ng, Kher Hui and Ryoichi Komiya. (2002) 'A global multimedia test-bed: Malaysia's Multimedia Super Corridor'. *2002 IEEE International Conference on Communications. Conference Proceedings. ICC 2002 (Cat. No.02CH37333), Communications, 2002* (4, p. 2459). doi:10.1109/ICC.2002.997285

Ng, See Kee and Bahiyah Omar. (2020) 'Web interactivity and news credibility: which is the stronger predictor to online news consumption in Malaysia?' *SEARCH Journal of Media and Communication Research*, The 6th International SEARCH Conference 2019, 89–106. Available online: www.researchgate.net/profile/ See-Kee-Ng/publication/343721412_Web_interactivity_and_news_credibility_ Which_is_the_stronger_predictor_to_online_news_consumption_in_Malay sia/links/5f3bd40b299bf13404cd75d3/Web-interactivity-and-news-credibil ity-Which-is-the-stronger-predictor-to-online-news-consumption-in-Malay sia.pdf

Nguyen, An. (2006) 'The status and relevance of Vietnamese journalism education: an empirical analysis'. *Asia Pacific Media Educator* 17 (December 2006): 41–55.

Nguyen, Nhat Nguyen, Nil Özçaglar-Toulouse and och Dannie Kjeldgaard. (2018) 'Toward an understanding of young consumers' daily consumption practices in post-Doi Moi Vietnam'. *Journal of Business Research* 86: 490–500.

Nguyen, Phúc Thùy Dương. (2014) 'From blog to Facebook – Your voice matter? An insight into the surge of citizen media in Vietnam'. Available online SSRN: https://ssrn.com/abstract=2526109

Nguyen, Qi. (2021) Vietnamese spend more time on internet, social media than Asian peers: report. Available online: https://e.vnexpress.net/news/news/ vietnamese-spend-more-time-on-internet-social-media-than-asian-peers-rep ort-4232155.html

Nguyen, Thoi. (2019) Vietnam's controversial cybersecurity law spells tough times for activists. Available online: https://thediplomat.com/2019/01/vietnams-controversial-cybersecurity-law-spells-tough-times-for-activists/

Nguyen-Thu, G. (2018) 'Vietnamese media going social: connectivism, collectivism, and conservatism'. *The Journal of Asian Studies* 77 (4): 895–908.

O'Connell, Mark. (2018, 19 December) 'The unnameable'. In Slate Magazine. Available online: https://slate.com/culture/2018/12/milkman-hooker-prize-novel-review.html (Accessed on 11 November 2021).

Omar, Bahiyah. (2014) 'Immediacy gratification in online news consumption and its relation to motivation, orientation and elaboration of news'. *Procedia: Social and Behavioral Sciences* 155 (i): 405–411.

Ott, Brian L. and Robert L. Mark. (2020) *Critical Media Studies: An Introduction*. 3rd ed. Hoboken, NJ: Wiley & Sons, Inc.

Pak, Jennifer. (2014) What is Malaysia's sedition law?, *BBC*, 27 November. Available online: www.bbc.com/news/world-asia-29373164

Pantti, Mervi and Karin Wahl-Jorgensen. (2021) 'Journalism and emotional work'. *Journalism Studies* 22 (12): 1567–1573.

Papacharissi, Zizi. (2014) *Affective Publics: Sentiment and the New Political*. New York: Oxford University Press.

Papacharissi, Zizi. (2021) *After Democracy: Imagining Our Political Future*. New Haven, CT: Yale University Press.

Park, Chang Sup. (2019) 'Does too much news on social media discourage news seeking? Mediating role of news efficacy between perceived news overload and news avoidance on social media'. *Social Media + Society* 5 (3): 1–12. doi:10.1177/2056305119872956Peck, Jamie. (2010) *Constructions of Neoliberal Reason*. Oxford: Oxford University Press.

Peck, Jamie. (2020) 'An interview with Jamie Peck'. In Simon Dawes and Marc Lenormand, eds. *Neoliberalism in Context: Governance, Subjectivity and Knowledge*. London: Palgrave Macmillan, pp. 289–308.

Pedwell, Carolyn. (2014) *Affective Relations: The Transnational Politics of Empathy*. London: Palgrave Macmillan.

Peters, Chris and Marcel Broersma, eds. (2017) *Rethinking Journalism Again*. London: Routledge.

Pettman, Dominic. (2016) *Infinite Distraction: Paying Attention to Social Media*. Cambridge: Polity Press.

Pew Research Center. (2004–2021) State of the News Media Project. Stateofthemedia.org

Pew Research Center. (2018) Publics globally want unbiased news coverage but are divided on whether their news media deliver. Available online: www.pewglo bal.org/2018/01/11/publics-globally-want-unbiased-news-coverage-but-are-divided-on-whether-their-news-media-deliver/

Pham, Linh. (2020) Vietnam hardens crackdown on toxic media content, with Facebook, Google concessions. Available online: http://hanoitimes.vn/viet nam-hardens-crackdown-on-toxic-media-content-with-facebook-google-conc essions-314634.html

Phelan, Sean. (2014) *Neoliberalism, Media and the Political*. Basingstoke: Palgrave.

Phillips, Whitney and Ryan M. Milner. (2017) *The Ambivalent Internet: Mischief, Oddity, and Antagonism Online*. Cambridge: Polity Press.

Pickard, Victor. (2019) *Democracy Without Journalism? Confronting the Misinformation Society*. New York: Oxford University Press.

Plantinga, Carl. (2018) *Screen Stories: Emotions and Ethics of Engagement*. Oxford: Oxford University Press.

Plummer, Ken. (2003) *Intimate Citizenship*. Seattle and London: University of Washington Press.

Pomerantsev, Peter. (2019) *This is Not Propaganda: Adventures in the War Against Reality*. London: Faber and Faber.

Przeworski, Adam. (2019) *Crises of Democracy*. Cambridge: Polity Press.

Putnam, Robert. (2000) *Bowling Alone: The Collapse and Revival of American Community*. New York: Simom & Schuster.

Reese, Stephen D. (2021) *The Crisis of the Institutional Press*. Cambridge: Polity Press.

Reuters. (2016) *Bersih 5: thousands march in Malaysian capital calling for PM Najib to step down* [Online]. Available at: www.cnbc.com/2016/11/19/ber sih-5-thousands-march-in-malaysian-capital-calling-for-pm-najib-to-step-down.html

Reuters. (2021a) 'Belarus jails opposition leader's husband for 18 years'. *The Guardian* 14 December. Available online: www.theguardian.com/world/2021/ dec/14/belarus-jails-opposition-leaders-husband-for-18-years

Reuters. (2021b) Vietnam journalists who criticised government jailed for 'spreading propaganda'. Available online: www.theguardian.com/world/2021/jan/06/vietnam-journalists-who-criticised-government-jailed-for-spreading-propaganda

Richardson, Kay, Katy Parry and John Corner. (2013) *Political Culture and Media Genre: Beyond News*. London: Palgrave Macmillan.

Rimmerman, Craig A. (2015) *The Lesbian and Gay Movements: Assimilation of Liberation?* 2nd ed. Boulder, CO: Westview Press.

Robbins, Mary Susannah. (2007) *Against the Vietnam War: Writings by Activists*. Lapham, MD: Rowman & Littlefield.

Rosa, Harmut. (2019) *Resonance: A Sociology of Our Relationship to the World* (trans. J Wagner). Cambridge: Polity Press.

Roser, Max and Bastian Herre. (2022) 'Democracy'. OurWorldinData.org Available online: https://ourworldindata.org/democracy

Roth, Andrew. (2021) 'The support group at the heart of Belarus' sporting resistance'. *The Guardian* 7 August. Available online: www.theguardian.com/world/2021/aug/07/the-support-group-at-the-heart-of-belaruss-sporting-resistance

Rouch, Jennifer. (2020) *Resisting the News: Engaged Audiences, Alternative Media and Popular Critique of Journalism*. London: Routledge.

Rukmalie, Jayakody and Pham Thi Thu Phuong. (2013) 'Social change and fathering: change or continuity in Vietnam?' *Journal of Family Issues* 34 (2): 228–249.

Sachs, Jeffrey D. (2012) 'Occupy global capitalism'. In Janet Byrne, ed. *The Occupy Handbook*. New York: Backbay Books/Little, Brown and Co, pp. 462–474.

Sakhnin, Alexei. (2021, 29 July) 'The opposition business'. *New Left Review*. Available online: https://newleftreview.org/sidecar/posts/the-opposition-business

Salleh, Mohammed. (2012) 'The impact of interactivity features in enhancing online communication satisfaction'. *Journal Komunikasi: Malaysian Journal of Communication* 28 (2): 21–36.

Sassatelli, Roberta. (2007) *Consumer Culture: History, Theory and Politics*. London: Sage.

Schofield Clark, Lynn S. and Regina Marchi. (2017) *Young People and the Future of News: Social Media and the Rise of Connective Journalism*, Cambridge: Cambridge University Press.

Seale, Clive, ed. (2012) *Qualitative Interviewing, from Researching Society and Culture*. London: Sage.

Seidman, Rachel F. (2019) *Speaking of Feminism: Today's Activities on the Past, Present and Future of the US Women's Movement*. Chapel Hill, NC: University of North Carolina Press.

Sharma, Devika and Fredrik Tygstrup, eds. (2015) *Structures of Feeling: Affectivity and the Study of Culture*. Munich and Boston: de Gruyter.

Shilling, Marcus. (2018) Interview with Annette Hill (October 2018). Lund, Sweden.

Shotter, James and Max Seddon. (2021) 'How Belarus' protesters staged a digital revolution'. *Financial Times* 21 February. Available online: www.ft.com/content/a68a1c28-fdd0-4800-9339-6ca1e81d456a

Shove, Elizabeth, Mike Pantzar and Matt Watson. (2012) *The Dynamics of Social Practice: Everyday Life and How it Changes*. London: Sage.

Siegien, Paulina and Wojciech Siegien. (2021) 'Between history and magic'. *New Eastern Europe* XLVII (5): 54–60.

Sierakowski, Slawomir. (2020) 'Belarus uprising: the making of a revolution'. *Journal of Democracy* 31 (4): 5–16. Available online: www.journalofdemocr acy.org/articles/belarus-uprising-the-making-of-a-revolution/

Silverstone, Roger. (1994) *Television and Everyday Life*. London: Routledge.

Sjparaga, Olga. (2021) 'Den belarusisk revolutionen lever vidare genom ömsesidig omsorg' (The Belariusian revolution lives on through mutual care). *Dagens nyheter* 4 August. Available online: www.dn.se/kultur/olga-sjparaga-den-bela rusiska-revolutionen-lever-vidare-genom-omsesidig-omsorg/

Snyder, Timothy. (2003) *The Reconstruction of Nations: Poland, Ukraine, Lithuania, Belarus 1569–1999*. New Haven, CT: Yale University Press.

Snyder, Timothy. (2011) *Bloodlands: Europe Between Hitler and Stalin*. New York: Vintage.

South China Morning Post. (2020) At Vietnam's 'Dong Tam Massacre', activists claim government attacked its own citizens. Available online: www.scmp. com/news/asia/southeast-asia/article/3046192/vietnams-dong-tam-massa cre-activists-claim-government

Statista. (2020) Number of internet users in Vietnam from 2017 to 2023. Available online: www.statista.com/statistics/369732/internet-users-vietnam/

Steensen, Steen, Raul Ferrer-Conill and Chris Peters. (2020) '(Against a) theory of audience engagement with news'. *Journalism Studies* 21 (12): 1662–1680.

Strotsev, Dimitrij. (2021) 'Belarus: motståndets konst' (Belarus: the art of resistance). In Ida Börjel and Mikael Nydahl, eds. *Ett år I Belarus. Röster inifrån en folkresning (One Year in Belarus: Voices From Within a Popular Uprising)*. Stockholm: Atlas, pp. 195–210.

Stulberg, Lisa M. (2016) *LGBTQ Social Movements*. Cambridge: Polity Press.

Sukumaran, Tashny. (2021) *Malaysia declares emergency over Covid-19 surge, giving embattled Muhyiddin some breathing room* [Online]. Available at: www. scmp.com/week-asia/health-environment/article/3117334/malaysian-king-declares-state-emergency-coronavirus

Sunstein, Cass. (2017) *#Republic: Divided Democracy in the Age of Social Media*. Princeton, NJ: Princeton University Press.

Swart, Joelle. (2021) 'Tactics of news literacy: how young people access, evaluate and engage with news on social media'. *New Media and Society* May 2021: 1–17.

Swart, Joëlle, Chris Peters and Marcel Broersma. (2017) 'Repositioning news and public connection in everyday life: a user-oriented perspective on inclusiveness, engagement, relevance, and constructiveness'. *Media, Culture & Society* 39 (6): 902–918.

Swart, Joëlle, Tim Groot Kormelink, Irene Costera Meijer and Marcel Broersma. (2022) 'Advancing a radical audience turn in journalism: fundamental dilemmas for journalism studies', *Digital Journalism* 10 (1): 8–22.

Syvertsen, Trine. (2020) *Digital Detox: The Politics of Disconnection*. Dublin: Emerald Publishing.

Tan, Eugene K.B. (2001) 'From sojourners to citizens: managing the ethnic Chinese minority in Indonesia and Malaysia'. *Ethnic & Racial Studies* 24 (6): 949–978.

Tan, Soon-Aun, Sarvarubini Nainee and Chee-Seng Tan. (2021) 'The mediating role of reciprocal filial piety in the relationship between parental autonomy support and life satisfaction among adolescents in Malaysia'. *Current Psychology* 40 (2): 804–812.

Taylor, Charles. (2004) *Modern Social Imaginaries*. London: Duke University Press.

Thomas, Elwyn. (1990) 'Filial piety, social change and Singapore youth'. *Journal of Moral Education* 19 (3): 192–205.

Tucker, Joshua A. (2021) 'Beyond liberation technology? The recent uses of social media by pro-democracy activists'. Project on Middle Est Political Science (POMEPS). https://pomeps.org/beyond-liberation-technology-the-recent-uses-of-social-media-by-pro-democracy-activists

Tumber, Howard and Silvio Waisbord, eds. (2021) *The Routledge Companion to Media Disinformation and Populism*. Abingdon: Routledge.

Turnbull, Sue. (2014) *TV Crime Drama*. Edinburgh: Edinburgh University Press.

Urbinati, Nadia. (2019) *Me the People: How Populism Transforms Democracy*. Cambridge, MA: Harvard University Press.

Uscinski, Joseph. (2020) *Conspiracy Theories: A Primer*. Lanham, MD: Rowman & Littlefield.

Vaidhyanathan, Siva. (2018) *Antisocial Media: How Facebook Disconnects Us and Undermines Democracy*. New York: Oxford University Press.

Van Duyn, Emily. (2022) *Democracy Lives in Darkness: How and Why People Keep Their Politics to Themselves*. New York: Oxford University Press.

Varna, Marius. (2020) 'Belarus protests: information control and technological censorship vs. connected societies'. Riga: NATO Strategic Communications Centre of Excellence, 8 December. Available online: https://stratcomcoe.org/cuploads/pfiles/belarus_protests_web_nato_stratcom_coe.pdf

Volodymyr, Artiukh. (2021) 'The anatomy of impatience: exploring the factors behind the 2020 labor unrest in Belarus'. *Slavic Review* 80 (1) 52–60.

Volkmer, Ingrid. (2014) *The Global Public Sphere*. Cambridge: Polity Press.

Walby, Sylvia. (2015) *Crisis*. London: Polity.

Wahl-Jorgensen, Karin. (2019) *Emotions, Media and Politics*. Cambridge: Polity Press.

Walker, Mason and Katerina Eva Matsa. (2021) 'News consumption across social media in 2021'. Pew Research Center, 20 September. Available online: www.pewresearch.org/journalism/2021/09/20/news-consumption-across-social-media-in-2021/

Walker, Shaun. (2020) 'The only way to stop violence': why protesters are unmasking Belarus police'. *The Guardian* 17 September. Available online: www.theguardian.com/world/2020/sep/17/the-only-way-to-stop-violence-why-protesters-are-unmasking-belarus-police

Walmsley, Ben. (2019) *Audience Engagement in the Performing Arts: a Critical Analysis*. London: Palgrave Macmillan.

Walvaart, Marleen te, Alexander Dhoest and Hilde Van den Bulck. (2019) 'Production perspectives on audience engagement: community building for current affairs television'. *Media Industries* 6 (1): 43–66.

Warner, Michael. (2002) *Publics and Counterpublics*. New York: Zone Books.

Webb, Amy. (2019) *The Big Nine: How the Tech Titans and their Thinking Machines Could Warp Humanity*. New York: PublicAffairs/Hachette Publishing.

Wells-Dang, Andrew. (2014) The political influence of civil society in Vietnam. In Jonathan London, ed. *Politics in Contemporary Vietnam*. Basingstoke: Palgrave Macmillan, pp. 162–183.

Wike, Richard and Janell Fetteroff. (2021) 'Global public opinion in an era of democratic anxiety'. Pew Research Center. Available online: www.pewresea rch.org/global/2021/12/07/global-public-opinion-in-an-era-of-democratic-anxiety/

Willems, Wendy. (2020) 'Beyond platform-centrism and digital universalism: the relational affordances of mobile social media publics'. *Information, Communication & Society* 24 (12): 1677–1693.

Williams, Raymond. (1977) *Marxism and Literature*. Oxford: Oxford University Press.

Williams, Sean. (2020) 'Belarus has torn up the protest rule book. Everyone should listen'. *WIRED*, 18 August. Available online: www.wired.co.uk/article/belarus-protests-telegram

Wilson, Andrew. (2021) *Belarus: The Last European Dictatorship*. rev. ed. New Haven, CT: Yale University Press.

Winiarski, Michael. (2021) 'Europa måste veta att vi lever som under en ockupation' (Europe must know that we live like under an occupation) *Dagens nyheter*, 5 (October): 14–15. Available online: www.dn.se/varlden/europa-maste-fa-veta-att-vi-lever-som-under-en-ockupation/

Wong, Kokkeong. (2004) 'Asian-based development journalism and political elections'. *Gazette: International Journal for Communication Studies* 66 (1): 25–40. doi:10.1177/0016549204039940

Wong, Vin Sy. (2019) Mapping the digital media publisher landscape in Vietnam. Available online: https://hashmeta.com/blog/mapping-the-digital-media-publisher-landscape-in-vietnam/

World Atlas. (2021) 'Languages spoken in Belarus'. Available online: www.worldatlas. com/articles/languages-spoken-in-belarus.html (Accessed on 1 December 2021).

World Bank. (2020a) Individuals using the internet (% of population) – Malaysia. Available online: https://data.worldbank.org/indicator/IT.NET.USER.ZS? locations=MY

World Bank. (2020b) Individuals using the internet (% of population) – Vietnam. Available online: https://data.worldbank.org/indicator/IT.NET.USER.ZS? locations=VN

World Bank. (2020c) The World Bank in Vietnam. Available online: www.worldbank. org/en/country/vietnam/overview#:~:text=According%20to%20the%202 019%20Population,region%20at%20similar%20income%20levels

Worldometer. (2020) Vietnam demographic. Available online: https://data.worldb ank.org/indicator/IT.NET.USER.ZS?locations=VN; www.worldometers.info/ demographics/vietnam-demographics/#pop (Accessed on 19 February 2021).

Yi, Tho Xin and Amir Yusof. (2021) *Muhyiddin Yassin appointed Malaysian caretaker PM after resignation is accepted by the king* [Online]. Available at: www.chan nelnewsasia.com/asia/malaysia-prime-minister-resign-muhyiddin-yassin- king-2115091

Yunus, Arfa. (2020) MP: don't repeal Sedition Act, amend it. *New Straits Times*, 13 August. Available online: www.nst.com.my/news/nation/2020/08/616356/ mp-dont-repeal-sedition-act-amend-it

Zinn, Howard. (2005/1980) *A People's History of the United States: 1492–Present.* New York: Harper Perennial Modern Classics.

Zuboff, Shoshana. (2019) *The Age of Surveillance Capitalism.* London: Profile Books.

Zulkafli, Nur Azimah, Bahiyah Omar and Nor Hazlina Hashim. (2014) Selective exposure to Berita Harian Online and Utusan Malaysia Online: the roles of surveillance motivation, website usability and website attractiveness. *SEARCH: The Journal of the South East Asia Research Centre for Communication and Humanities* 6 (2): 1–21.

INDEX

Note: Use of *italics* indicates an illustration on that page.

For Product Safety Concerns and Information please contact our EU
representative GPSR@taylorandfrancis.com
Taylor & Francis Verlag GmbH, Kaufingerstraße 24, 80331 München, Germany